CHICAGO
THE BEAUTIFUL

CHICAGO the Beautiful
A CITY REBORN

KENAN HEISE

Bonus Books, Inc.
Chicago

05   04   03   02   01

5   4   3   2   1

Library of Congress Control Number: 2001094617
ISBN: 1-56625-164-8

Bonus Books, Inc.
160 East Illinois Street
Chicago, IL 60611

Printed in the United States of America

*To all who help to make Chicago
ever more beautiful.*

▐ TABLE OF CONTENTS

THE BEAUTY OF THE CHICAGO WILDERNESS

CHICAGO TREASURES

▌Acknowledgments

Among the people who have contributed to this book are:

The Chicago Tourism Bureau's Cheryl Slaughter;

The Chicago Department of Environment, including Commissioner William F. Abolt, as well as Jessica Rio and Mark Farina;

From the Chicago Park District, Superintendent David Doig and Chief of Staff Drew Becher, as well as Angelynne Amores and Brook Collins;

Staff, board and volunteer members of
     The Friends of the Park,
     The Lake Michigan Federation,
     The Friends of the Chicago River,
     The Illinois Chapter of the Nature Conservancy;

Debra Shore of *Chicago Wilderness*;

The Chicago Audubon Society, especially Jerry Garden and Alan Anderson;

Marcia Webster-Davis of NeighborSpace;

Former Chicago alderman Leon Despres;

The Chicago Botanic Garden's Bridget Kellens Bittman;

The Morton Arboretum's Meredith Zelewsky;

The staff of the Klehm Arboretum and Botanic Garden;

The staffs of the forest preserves of Will, DuPage and Lake Counties, and of the McHenry County Conservation District;

Deputy Commissioner James Peters, Meredith Taussig and the entire staff of the Commission on Chicago Landmarks;

Eileen Keribar of Owings, Skidmore & Merrill LLP

Richard Cahan of City 2000;

Artist Scott Holingue;

UIC Special Collection's Pat Bakunas

Fran and John Eck;

George Lambros;

Steinkamp/Ballogg Photography;

Hedrich Blessing Photography;

Chicago CartoGraphics' Dennis McClendon;

Diane Korling.

A note of personal appreciation from the author to the individuals at Bonus Books whose talents and diligence have helped make this a beautiful book.

▌INTRODUCTION

The greatest and most nearly beautiful city of our young nation is probably Chicago. Eventually, I think that Chicago will be the most beautiful city left in the modern world.

—FRANK LLOYD WRIGHT, LONDON, 1939

We are born. We relate to beauty. We die.

Sometimes, as we reflect on life, it seems that simple.

Even if it is not, beauty remains an elusive reality, something we merely touch in our pursuit of life and the good.

This book has been written because now, in the twenty-first century, Frank Lloyd Wright's prediction is coming true. Beauty is indeed growing in and around Chicago and the world is taking notice.

More than 100 organizations from this area have banded together to preserve and develop the natural beauty of the region, which they now call "the Chicago Wilderness." The impact of this alliance has been an unprecedented rediscovery of and appreciation for a shared natural heritage.

The good news begins with an astonishing 250,000 to 300,000 new trees and a plethora of flowers throughout Chicago as well as the restoration and enhancement of the city's greatest jewels—its one-of-a-kind public lakefront and river.

Volunteers by the thousands are helping to plant trees and flowers, guide the lakefront improvements, restore the Chicago River, reseed tallgrass prairies, lead bird walks, interpret at local museums, explain the Loop's architecture and battle to save the highly polluted Lake Calumet area.

Even a decade ago, this could not have happened. A new spirit has spread throughout the region, opening Chicagoans' eyes to the beauty around them. Whatever the reasons, people today are finding ways to prove they care.

The Chicago Botanic Garden to the north of the city, for example, now has 43,000 members and more than 800 volunteers. In the poorest of Chicago neighborhoods, residents are taking horticultural classes and planting gardens of vegetables and flowers. To the southwest of Chicago, more than 600 volunteers are committed to a long-term project to restore the Midewin National Tallgrass Prairie. Already, they have received three top awards from the National Forest Service for their efforts.

News stories and word-of-mouth accounts by visitors to the region are spreading the story of Chicago and the surrounding area around the world.

Chicago the Beautiful seeks to bring together many diverse happenings in the area under one unifying aspect: their relationship to its growing beauty.

If one leader has inspired this aesthetic rebirth, he is Chicago Mayor Richard M. Daley. He has earned recognition and respect for making ambitious beautification efforts happen—and for not excluding the poor, minorities or even the residents of suburbs beyond his political realm.

In the final analysis, however, it is the people who are saying "yes" to the metropolitan area's billion-dollar transformation.

More than ever, the high aspirations and determined efforts of planners, professionals and volunteers make clear that, ultimately, the most beautiful aspect of Chicago is its people.

The New Splendor of

CHICAGO

I. Throughout CHICAGO:
NEW TREES & FLOWERS

THE TREES

> *The greatest contribution of trees to people is subtle and funda-*
> *mental. . . . They sustain our soil, moderate out climate, con-*
> *serve our water, cool our streets and soften the edges of our lives.*

—FROM A MORTON ARBORETUM BROCHURE

The numbers are astonishing. Upwards of 250,000 (some say 300,000) trees have been planted across the city in a little more than a decade. Chicago has been transformed.

With the change has come new beauty, a welcoming sign on behalf of the city.

Once, a visitor could look up or down any street in the Loop and see only people, cars, sidewalks and buildings. Now, the new flowers and trees sneak into the picture the way the half smile does on the Mona Lisa.

The impact?

- The new trees, like subtle jewelry, enhance an already beautiful city.
- The air, refreshed moment by moment with greater quantities of tree-manufactured oxygen, has become healthier.
- The city's famous architecture, exciting and eye-catching, is now framed with greenery.
- Chicago's wind, legendary and at times annoying, now braces itself against masses of leaves.
- The migratory birds who use the lake and area rivers as flyways or reference points find new perches, shelter and food in the additional trees.
- The cement and asphalt, catch-alls for summer heat, are cooler now.
- Finally, Chicago, the hustling and bustling city, slows down a little to experience the new plant life and birds.

More than a decade has passed since the first new trees were planted. The city remains astounded. Chicago likes its abundant foliage.

The trees are found even under the elevated Dan Ryan Expressway. In the Pilsen neighborhood, on a little plot of land east of Halsted and south of 21st Street, stands a tiny "forest" of white pines and Douglas fir trees. They are located in a jungle of cement, overhead of which roars the traffic of the pillared highway. Their only neighbors are side streets, fences and billboards.

Trees have been planted in the city's parks, along its streets and in the meridians of major thoroughfares, including Lake Shore Drive. The trees

HOW THE TREES CAME TO BE PLANTED

All these changes began in the early 1990s. The city administration, spearheaded by Mayor Richard M. Daley, started adding trees on a scale that has taxed nurseries for hundreds of miles around.

His stated goal was 500,000 new trees for Chicago.

Daley, who was born on Arbor Day, budgeted an additional $10 million for planting trees.

bring not only a fresh beauty, clean air and an extra friendliness to the city's public places, but also a new pride to Chicago.

In 1999, not satisfied with the trees planted by the city and the Chicago Park District, the mayor pushed through an ordinance requiring contractors to place at least one tree on every 25 feet of property frontage around newly constructed commercial buildings and renovated parking lots.

MORE THAN 47 SPECIES

The city's new trees represent more than 47 species. Among them are honeylocusts, green ashes, gingkoes, firs, oaks, lindens, the popular ash and the Kentucky coffee tree, which is tolerant of poor drainage and salt.

To his call for more trees, Daley then added another for certain buildings to cover their walls with ivy, a decoration in the tradition of the outfield walls of Chicago's Wrigley Field.

The mayor believes the new trees and greenery will discourage crime and vandalism, and help make Chicago a safer city.

TreeKeepers

The many trees planted throughout Chicago are maintained not only by the Bureau of Forestry and the Park District but also increasingly through an organization known as TreeKeepers. These are volunteers, citizen foresters. They receive training to give the trees the care and maintenance needed in what a recruitment brochure calls "an urban forest."

Participants in the TreeKeepers program commit themselves to volunteer for 24 hours "of community greening each year."

TreeKeeper Richard Booze explained his reason for getting involved:

Trees and the Picasso at Daley Plaza (City of Chicago/ Willy Schmidt)

The effort I devote to trees will bear fruit later. My grandchildren will say, "Granddad took care of that tree so it's here for everyone to enjoy." What a sweet reward for so little effort!

Forest trees may live hundreds of years, but ones in the city tend to survive a much shorter time. Thousands die annually from disease, stress, abuse and neglect. While Bureau of Forestry and Park District employees are the trees' primary caregivers, the Tree-Keepers' job is to help keep them green and growing.

The city has an estimated four million trees, which provide the TreeKeepers with an almost limitless challenge.

The Asian Long-Horned Beetle

You feel terrible when you find one.

—ANDY ELLIOTT, WHO HUNTED
THE TREE-DESTROYING BEETLES

Chicago's trees face a fearsome nemesis and its name is the Asian long-horned beetle. This critter potentially could destroy large numbers of them, a fact that those who care about the environment fully realize.

While this dangerous beetle has not yet been eradicated, an army of scientists, foresters, volunteers as well as federal and local employees seem to have it tentatively in check.

The most successful tactic in the fight to eliminate the Asian long-horned beetles has been to remove any tree that was or might have been infected.

When someone spots what they believe to be an Asian long-horned (rather than the common, similar brown) beetle, the scientists test the

ONE SOLUTION

In China, two beetles have been identified that will kill the Asian long-horned, but the more effective one also kills the honeybees of the area, destroying one of the most helpful insects in American agriculture.

The first discovery of an Asian long-horned beetle was on the North Side in a tree on the 4400 block of Winchester Avenue. It was during July 1998. The beetle, which originated in China, is believed to have reached Chicago nesting comfortably in a crate or other product made of wood.

tree or trees by listening for the unique sound of the immigrant critter boring through the wood.

If scientists find that a tree is infested, it is then destroyed forthwith and all neighboring trees are checked.

Within two years after the first such beetle was spotted, more than 1,300 trees had to be destroyed in the city and suburbs.

Most of these, however, were eradicated in the first year and a half.

What would have happened had the beetle immigrated to Chicago a quarter or half century ago? Would the science have been strong enough then to fight the Asian long-horned beetle—and would Chicagoans have been concerned enough to fight it?

The Chicago area remains concerned. The city has grown to like its trees.

F L O W E R S   &   G A R D E N S

City in a garden.

—CHICAGO'S MOTTO, ADOPTED IN 1837

Chicago now has flowers and gardens, vast and beautiful expanses of them, all over. They are rich with color and variety, and can often be found in surprising locations:

URBS IN HORTO FUND

Urbs in Horto ("City in a Garden") is the motto of Chicago and also the name of a fund initiated by the city and administered by the Community Trust. Through it, a variety of different organizations can apply for "public greening grants" that range from $250 to $10,000. Eligible recipients include schools, libraries, churches, civic clubs and public housing organizations.

Medians on Michigan Avenue (City of Chicago/ Peter J. Schulz)

- Flowers in a great profusion now greet Chicago residents and visitors in the Loop as well as along all the various expressways, train routes and highways in and out of the city.

- The neighborhoods are full of colorful plantings in small back yards, on once ugly and abandoned lots as well as in dividers in the center of avenues such as Ashland, Western and Jackson.

- Visitors can see flowers at the exits as they drive away from the O'Hare International and Midway Airports.

- Flowers wave in the breeze from planters on the overpasses along Lake Shore Drive. They hang in baskets from lightpoles throughout Chicago.

- They are on the first floor windowsills of City Hall, the Cultural Center and other public buildings.

- The banks of railroad tracks heading into the city abound with well-cultivated patches of flowers.

- They gloriously bedeck North Michigan Avenue in the median and along the sidewalks.

- Each year, over the past decade, more and more empty neighborhood lots have been transformed into gardens with flowers as well as vegetables.

- As never before, commercial structures in and around the Loop, and homes and office buildings throughout the Chicago area show them in flowerboxes, pots, and in small patches of land adjacent to the structures.

- The University of Chicago and the Park District have turned the Midway Plaisance into an outdoor conservatory, using ideas proposed in the nineteenth century by landscape architect Fredrick Law Olmstead.

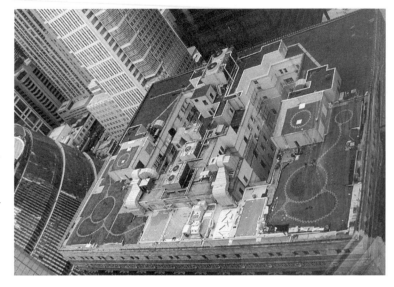

City Hall Rooftop Garden

Often the greatest beauty lies off the beaten path. Certainly, a garden perched on the top of a Chicago building is such. Creative plots on the roof of City Hall were designed, and the first tree was planted in the year 2000. It is hoped this garden will serve as a model for other buildings in the Loop and throughout Chicago's neighborhoods.

Planted in an imaginative geometric pattern, the City Hall roof garden is visible from the office windows of many nearby skyscrapers.

ON TAR ROOFS, TREES AND FLOWERS

Work on the City Hall rooftop garden could be glimpsed through a 25th floor window at 30 North LaSalle Street during an interview with Chicago environmental commissioner William Abolt. The commissioner explained to the author the thinking that helped create the City Hall rooftop gardens.

"Through the Nature Chicago programs," he said, "we want to make places prettier and people happier. It is that simple. This garden also will cool down this urban heat island and help air quality."

He sees the garden on top of City Hall and others being planted elsewhere on Loop buildings as "a scientific experiment."

"Old black tar roofs retain heat just as dark clothing does," he said. "We want to study the difference it might make in people's lives by replacing heat-retaining roofs with actual gardens. How much new green space would be needed to cool the city down by a measurable degree? Also, how will waste water be affected when plants absorb more water and there is no run-off? How will replacing a tar roof with a garden affect pollution and air quality in the city? We are going to test and find out."

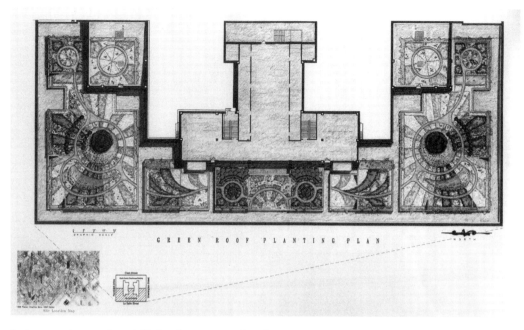

GREEN ROOF PLANTING PLAN

It is amazing and a delight that not only plants survive on the roof of City Hall; moths, butterflies, birds, bees and other insects—even dragonflies—also find their way there. A hand placed near or on the greenery on a hot day finds the spot noticeably cooler than the air a foot or two above the flowers.

City Hall Rooftop Garden design (Chicago Department of Environment)

This garden, though not open to the public, yet belongs to it and contributes to the commonweal.

Gateway Green

Gateway Green, another beautification program for the city, is a partnership established between Chicago and the State of Illinois to clean up and landscape the various routes into and out of the city.

For contributing anywhere from $5,000 to $100,000, a corporate sponsor can get credit for planting and maintaining a plot along a major route that brings people into Chicago. The money is used to hire landscapers to do the work.

The reward for the corporate entity is name reinforcement—a sign with the corporation's name on it in an area where billboards are strictly forbidden.

Not all are happy with the execution of this idea. Joanne Trestrail wrote in the *Chicago Tribune:*

It's the signs. What's with the signs?

You've seen them. In each case, there are two, stacked one on top of the other on a post. The top, oval has a big leaf on it. The bottom, squarish one credits a sponsor.

Your first thought is: What's that? Your second: That leaf's not as bad as it could be. Your third, or my third: Why do I have to look at these?

Talk about alloyed pleasure. If the signs were anywhere but along the expressways, they'd merge with the rest of the visual clutter and few people would care.

Community Gardeners

Profusion and colorful variety are only half of the story of the city's flowers. The people responding to this new initiative are the second half. While the city has planted bulbs, seeds and vases of flowers, it has been no less active in encouraging citizens and organizations to do the same on their own.

Many Chicagoans who have scarcely even attempted to pot a plant are becoming gardeners and taking courses to learn the kind of soil and seeds to use for specific species of flowers and trees.

Chicago is not the only urban area to become flower conscious or to choose exotic places to plant them. Cities, especially those in the Northwest, are encouraging the additional use of flowers and gardens to beautify streets and renew neighborhoods. None, however, has been anywhere near as aggressive, persistent and enthusiastic as Chicago is.

One has to go to Europe, specifically to England, to find Chicago's equal.

NeighborSpace

Through its NeighborSpace program, Chicago continues to buy unused lots and turn them over to community control for the development of gardens.

NeighborSpace was incorporated in mid-1996 with the avowed intention of acquiring land for gardening. By the turn of the century, it had received recognition and financial support from city, state and national groups, and had more than doubled the initial number of cultivated plots of land.

In a joint effort, the city, county and forest preserves district then renewed the initial three-year program for 20 more years, with funding to be appropriated on an annual basis.

Many of the gardens, located all over the city, can be found in offbeat places, clustered along railroad tracks or on sidelots in poorer inner city neighborhoods.

Frequently, these gardens are growing produce as well as flowers.

JoElla Williams, who set to work with zeal on the 3800 West Flourney Block Club Community Garden, told an interviewer:

> The garden is like a doctor. When I put a plant out there with my hands and see it come back next year, it makes me want to live.

The explosion of flowers that has changed Chicago over the last decade has included training community gardeners in the basic and extended science of growing and tending plants, in other words, horticulture.

The new flower gardeners have quickly learned the names of various plants, how to choose the right ones for a given place, garden design, proper maintenance and the creation of ever new possibilities and approaches to growing flowers.

Greencorps Chicago

The City of Chicago is aware of the need for support to assist citizens in growing gardens. It has responded with Greencorps, a program of the city's Department of Environment.

WHY THEY CALL IT "PARADISE"

The Paradise Garden in Austin replaced an abandoned 24-unit building that had taken Austin residents six years of complaining to have torn down.

The stated purpose of Greencorps Chicago is "To enable Chicagoans to improve the quality of life in their neighborhoods by providing horticultural instruction, materials and employment."

By assisting more than 500 community groups throughout the city to "green" their neighborhoods, Greencorps has enabled citizen gardeners to become both active and effective.

Greencorps has five programs:

1. *Greencorps Chicago Crew Jobs for Unemployed Chicagoans:* Unemployed individuals can acquire horticultural skills training by working with community groups to carry out their gardening projects. These workers are matched with local committed and trained volunteers.

2. *Comprehensive Help:* Workshop staff assistance and funding is available for any community organizations which commit themselves to having at least two members attend five three-hour workshops. Participants are trained in horticulture, garden design and volunteer recruitment. Working with a staff of horticulturists and Greencorps crews, community gardeners lay out and install trees, shrubs, perennials, vines, arbors and benches.

3. *Basic Assistance and One Day of Onsite Aid:* These are provided to groups which are not able to pledge themselves to such a large project. This help can be used to prepare a site or enhance a garden that already exists.

4. *Citywide Distribution Days:* The program distributes seeds, bulbs and plants to community gardeners. These include annual and perennial flowers as well as vegetables, most of them donated by local garden centers.

5. *School Initiative.* Through this program, students can help to design or install a garden or perform landscaping at their school as part of their service learning hours—the community service requirement that both public and parochial school students must complete as part of their education.

When Greencorps began, its aid was limited to gardening, but it has since expanded into new areas of job training, including recycling/pollution prevention, brownfields remediation and river restoration.

These efforts are beginning to root themselves as deeply into the fabric of the city as the trees and flowers themselves.

2. The CHICAGO RIVER:
A VISION OF AN AMERICAN VENICE

The rivers are our brothers. They quench our thirst. The rivers carry our canoes, and feed our children. If we sell you our land, you must remember and teach your children that the rivers are our brothers, and yours. And you must henceforth give the rivers the kindness you give any brother.

—SEATTLE, CHIEF OF THE SUQUAMISH TRIBE

A WATERWAY AMID SKYSCRAPERS

The Chicago River has long been a distantly admired but underappreciated feature of the city.

Now, however, Chicagoans want to restore a youthful vitality to the river, both downtown and throughout its neighborhood meanderings. They have started to make changes, which are giving the river and the city a surprising new face—a beautiful, easy-to-smile-at one.

If all these plans for restoration continue, Chicago's waterway might well give the city the appearance of an American Venice, complete with not only gondolas but also hanging flowers and barges full of musicians.

The 1909 *Plan of Chicago,* the city's urban renewal plan of almost a century ago, called for the river's banks to be restored to the public "for the pleasure of the people."

"Restored" is a precise word. From the beginning, these banks were supposed to be public, to belong to the citizens of Chicago.

In 1830, three years before the settlement even became a village, James Thompson surveyed it and created a plan for Chicago in the form of a

The bend in the river (City of Chicago/ Peter J. Schulz)

grid. He stipulated in drafting it that the banks of the river were to stay public.

In 1912, historian J. Seymour Currey reflected on Thompson's plan and the fate of those riverbanks in a land-hungry city:

> It was found expedient in later years, however, to abandon this [Thompson's] plan and the ground was eventually sold and built upon.

A city with an accessible public river running through it could have been so very different from one whose waterway was not available to and enjoyed by its people.

In Daniel Burnham's amply illustrated *Plan of Chicago,* no images are presented with more verve and imaginative detail than its proposals for the banks of river. Probably because they were partially acted upon, the suggestions for the lakefront are more often considered the key to that plan. The drawings themselves, however, give reason to argue that the river was the pivotal point of the new look envisioned for Chicago.

Early 1900s postcard view of the Chicago River

Burnham's plan, at its core, had tried to restore both the river and the lakefront to the people. Currey, writing three years later in 1912, was confident that the river restoration would happen.

It did not. Not yet. But now, at the start of the twenty-first century, the intent of the original surveyor of Chicago is finally becoming reality.

Spurred in the last 25 years by Friends of the Chicago River and other citizens interest groups, the city conceived and has started work on a list of surprising changes.

These changes would outdo even the *Plan of Chicago's* vision for the river. The city is restoring the beauty of the riverbanks, not with architectural ornamentation, but with flowers, shrubs, ivy and trees. It has set out to make its river accessible to its people as a recreational waterway, with stairways, a walkway, shops, restaurants and a public plaza.

These changes should greatly refocus the image of the city itself—like rare jade in the center of a crown.

Earlier Restoration Efforts

The river, long polluted and unavailable to the public was a standing joke in Chicago.

In his 1942 book, *The Chicago,* Harry Hansen quoted a friend's assessment of the river:

What is it but a creek that doesn't know which way to go? Sometimes, it flows south, and sometimes it flows north; on some days it has to be regulated by pumps and others it stagnates and gets covered with a scum of bottle green. The city could have filled it up long ago and made a fine parkway out of it, and everybody would have been better served.

In the river's defense, Hansen argued that the city had owed its very existence to the river. Its main channel, he pointed out, "was never navigable for more than five or six miles, but those miles were the key to the lock that opened the treasure of a continent."

Hansen, in a more realistic assessment, listed the words which people used to describe the river, from "channel" to "ditch" and ending with "sewer."

Even in more recent years, Chicagoans could identify with Hansen's use of the word "sewer" as they watched downtown drainpipes empty filth into the river, especially the runoff from unswept streets after a rain.

The condition of the Chicago River first began to improve measurably in the early 1960s with efforts by the Metropolitan Sanitary District of Greater Chicago (now, the Water Reclamation District of Greater Chicago) to clean it up.

Vinton Bacon, then executive director of the district, publicly envisioned a day when people would be fishing and water-skiing on the river. Because his goals seemed so unattainable, he was called a dreamer and ridiculed. Not even carp, it was said, could survive in the Chicago River.

DIVERS BEWARE: THE RIVER COULD GET YOU

When a police marine unit officer or a firefighter dived into the Chicago River to recover anyone or anything in years gone by, he then had to go through strict and elaborate sanitary procedures as a follow-up. These included a mandatory trip to Cook County Hospital and a tetanus shot.

Even to this day, police diving trainees are reminded of the police officer who jumped into the river to save a man. The rescued individual recovered but the rescuer had to spend six months in the hospital because of a mysterious bacterial infection. All anyone had to do was look at the surface of the water to see why.

Veteran divers today, however, remark how much better visibility they are encountering in both the lake and the river than they did earlier in their careers.

The main sources of pollution, however, were cut off one by one as a result of lawsuits and legal enforcement.

With new construction along the riverbanks in the 1970s and 1980s, the city initiated efforts to create a riverwalk with trees, bushes, flowers and an occasional bench on which to stop and rest. The latter was especially necessary because any user of the path constantly had to go up and down stairs to bypass bridge abutments.

The city also began a costly, ongoing program to rebuild the ugly, worn-out Loop-area bridges. It was especially expensive and time-consuming for the Lake Street Bridge, the second tier of which carries the moving Red Line "L" trains. Replacing individual bridges, which has taken up to two years per bridge, has made them safer and so much more beautiful.

The river path plan continued, and even the pedestrian, former Municipal Court building on the north side of the river managed to add an overhanging walkway along the water between Clark and LaSalle Streets.

A Water Reclamation District boat began routinely cleaning the surface of the water of any debris.

Next, several restaurants opened up at river level and provided views not only of the waterway and its traffic but also of the city's innovative architecture in the background.

The city's commuters learned they could travel by boats between the Magnificent Mile's Michigan Avenue Bridge and the Northwestern (now, the Union Pacific) Railroad and Union stations. Next, a variety of sightseeing and charter boat companies started offering tours out onto the lake as well as up and down the river.

A New Plan for the River

In 1990, a coalition representing Friends of the Chicago River and the city's Department of Planning established benchmark guidelines for returning the river to the public and restoring its full beauty.

Using these guidelines, the city developed an ambitious vision that stunned its residents. It called, for example, for engineers to move Upper and Lower Wacker Drive with its support pillars back away from the water so the people of Chicago could have easier access to the river.

Chicago River adorned with flowers, with the Marina Towers in the background (City of Chicago/Mark Montgomery)

A SECOND LAKEFRONT

"The river," Mayor Richard Daley said in a *Chicago Wilderness* magazine interview, "could be . . . like a second lakefront. We're working to improve the river. Already, the water quality is better and now we're buying land and doing setbacks. The river will be comparable [to the lakefront] for nature and recreation."

The dreams of surveyor James Thompson and city planner Daniel Burnham were becoming reality. But from where would the money come to develop the river?

Taxes resulting from Chicago's prosperity would provide a major source. Federal dollars were requested and became available. In addition, the city came up with a plan. Funds budgeted for promoting the area as a place to visit could be shifted to projects such as enhancing the Chicago River. Thus, deeds rather than words would be used to attract tourists.

The first dramatic step was a privately developed walkway accessible to the public on the north side of the river going east from the Michigan Avenue Bridge. A wide and elegant stairway curved down to the water and seemed at first more than what was necessary as the pathway itself did not go far and was little used. It would take almost a decade for this walkway to reach out another half mile toward the lake.

Even then, the short pathway became a special place to some. A young architect, Michael Barnes, was traveling across the country on a fellowship to identify "urban retreats," places in the middle of cities where people could get away for a breather and reflection. This walkway was the Chicago spot he chose to list and photograph.

THE "ROMANCE IS BACK" ALONG A REVITALIZED RIVER.

From an August 20, 2000 "Chicago Journal" column in the *New York Times*:

Indeed, the [floating pedal] bikes, the gondolas, the open-air cafes and the planters bursting with purple pansies are just the beginning of a multi-million-dollar construction plan, inspired by city's mayor, Richard J. Daley, to turn what has been a polluted industrial waterway into a gleaming tourist attraction. Among other things, the plan calls for a continuous, grassy pathway along the river, dozens of new cafes, canoe rental stands and more docks offering access to the river.

The largest new development along the banks was the reconstruction of Lower Wacker Drive, which runs parallel to the river. Previously, the pathway along the riverbank at Lower Wacker was narrow and interrupted by bridge encasements. By abbreviating the width of the drive, setbacks could be constructed along the south bank that made the riverwalk more accessible, more useful and more beautiful.

The river enhancement plans also added a Wabash Street public plaza at water level; a grand, sweeping stairway down to water level at the bend in the river; overhangs with shops, cafes and restaurants under them from Lake Street to the lake; and river walkway extensions to circumvent the wide bridge abutments.

Restoration and beauty were not enough for the Chicago River, however. The mayor and his planners conceived another: romance.

In 2000, to herald the new image of the river, they imported gondoliers to ply the river as they do the canals in Venice.

For do-it-yourself people, the city offered pedaled waterbikes on the river.

Additional plans called for barges filled with musicians to serenade those eating or strolling along the river in the downtown areas as well as at neighborhood locations along the North and South branches.

At Wabash and the river, a plaza was designed to stage large-scale musical performances as well as other public events, adding a new mix of theatricality and charm to the river's image.

These, along with the flowers, shrubbery and trees, have transformed the long-time cement-and-debris look of the Chicago River into a panorama of beauty. Meanwhile, more and more shops and restaurants have added a commercial quaintness to the river's banks.

Still, even with all these improvements, there is reason to believe that the best might be yet to come.

THE CHICAGO RIVER SYSTEM: THE FRONT YARD OF THE CITY

Many say the river has become a symbol of how the city has changed from a gritty meat-packing town to a vibrant, clean city of art museums, neighborhood festivals and outdoor restaurants.

—THE NEW YORK TIMES, AUG. 20, 2000

The Chicago area is in the midst of discovering the river, the complete 150 miles of its trunk, branches and forks.

Unraveling a piece of geography generally requires a map. The rediscovery of the Chicago River system has long called for a detailed one.

This chart now exists. It comes in the form of a book by David M. Solzman, *The Chicago River: An Illustrated History and Guide to the River and Its Waterways* (Wild Onion Books, 1998).

"The largest part of the book," its introduction explains, "contains a series of waterway tours. Each tour is broken into sections; a map and detailed text describe the history, character and points of interest of each section."

These maps are treasures for not only the canoeist or hiker, but also the residents of the various neighborhoods through which the river winds its way. The book and its charts are laced with local history, detailed reports of ecological developments, and the names of shuttered factories. The pages also include complaints about local abuses of the river and give descriptions of the prairies and wetlands along with running commentary and meaningful stories.

Accounts weave throughout the book of the various individuals and groups who "have worked assiduously to reverse the decline of the waterway."

Its publication came at a fortunate time, with the city scheduling restoration that has included canoe launches to connect Lake Michigan, the river and Lake Calumet.

The maps note areas along the river that have been preserved by various conservation groups and local community organizations. They tell of improvements made by homeowners, businesses and the City of Chicago.

GOOSE ISLAND

This island on the North Branch of the Chicago River covers 160 acres, the size of an average farm in the Midwest. Irish immigrants noted for raising geese originally settled it. Hence, it received its nickname.

Harry Hansen wrote in *The Chicago:*

"Everybody had geese. The geese patrolled the streets and alleys and waddled down to the river's bank. Over 500 Irish families lived on this neck of land before the factories came."

The book provides a baseline for what is yet to come and reports on a major struggle along the river between gentrification and industrial preservation.

A second monumental book, *The Chicago River: A Natural and Unnatural History* (Lake Claremont Press, 2000), has been written by Libby Hill. She successfully combines historical scholarship with elegant prose.

Among the book's features are:

- a chronology of the river;
- a history that cites primary sources such as Chicago newspaper articles from the 1850s and suburban papers from the early 1900s;
- maps of the river and the Deep Tunnel Project; and
- scholarship backed up with good footnotes.

The author tells the story of the Chicago River, and she does it well.

The North Branch

A recent study by the Urban Land Institute designated the meandering North Branch of the Chicago River as the unifying aspect of the Northwest Side of Chicago, calling it "a salient neighborhood feature affording significant beauty and recreational opportunities."

The institute, in conclusion, urged new thinking about the river and suggested that the people who live along its banks start thinking of it as Chicago's "front yard" rather than its "back yard."

As Chicagoans along the North Branch increase their appreciation for the river, however, they continue to be caught up in the struggle between industry and the forces of gentrification. A classic example has been the fight over Goose Island on the Near Northwest Side of the city, between Chicago and North Avenues. A company owned by William B. Ogden, who had been Chicago's first mayor, created this island in the mid-1800s. The firm dug out what became a channel in order to get clay to make bricks.

On the perimeter of the island are such city, industrial and commercial ventures as the Department of Sanitation's 42nd Ward Yard, Waste Management, International Salt, Federal Express and the Greyhound Bus Company garage. Around the outside, add the Cabrini-Green Homes, the *Chicago Tribune* Freedom Center (printing presses), the AAA Boat Yard and the buildings that formerly housed the headquarters of Montgomery Ward & Co.

Yet just to the north lies one of the most gentrified residential sections of Chicago.

The center of Goose Island has been only slightly impacted by this gentrification. It is marked with factories, a carwash, a "gentleman's club" and a horseracing parlor—but no homes. A request to rezone a section of the island from industrial to residential was turned down and the area and corresponding riverbanks were declared an industrial zone.

(The city determined, nevertheless, that Goose Island should have a canoe launch.)

With the pressure of radical gentrification to the north, what could have happened to Goose Island if the rezoning had been approved? Some speculate the area might have become a secured enclave for the very wealthy.

Between Argyle and Foster, the north section of the river divides into the North Shore Channel and the North Branch. The West Fork of it splits off south of Golf Road with the North Branch being created by a juncture of the Middle Fork and the Skokie River.

All along these waterways are homes, schools, plants, institutions, prairies, wetlands, golf courses, cemeteries, woods and parks. They represent an ecological system strong and fragile, both scarred and extraordinarily beautiful.

THE RIVER BECOMES A SCHOOL

The city and the U.S. Army Corps of Engineers are working to stabilize the river's banks, enhance its habitats, increase recreational use and set up four model sites for learning about the river's ecosystem.

The North Channel

The North Channel runs eight miles from around Lawrence Avenue to an outlet into Lake Michigan that can be opened at Wilmette. It was dug in 1909 to supplement the Chicago Sanitary and Ship Canal, to help reverse the Chicago River and save Lake Michigan from tremendous pollution problems. The channel allows water to be pumped into the river and canal. It also has afforded boat owners an inlet harbor at Wilmette.

The North Channel contains one of the most beautiful stretches of the Chicago River system—that of Legion Park from Foster Avenue north to Peterson Avenue. It presents a rugged example of nature, with verdant banks and a lush overhang of trees. The viewer might indeed wonder whether he or she is actually within the corporate limits of one most populous cities of the world.

Farther north along the channel, the Skokie Northshore Sculpture Park offers not only a strip of well-tended park land but also dozens of interspersed pieces of public art by area artists. These often surprising works line a several-mile–long public walking and cycling path between the channel and McCormick Boulevard. The latter is named after Col. Robert R. McCormick, the eccentric publisher of the *Chicago Tribune.* He had headed the Metropolitan Sanitary District in the early years of the twentieth century, when it created the North Channel. His biographers, even the critical ones, credit him with having done a superb job supervising and facilitating the construction.

The channel is often hidden from those using the fast-moving boulevard. One place to stop and appreciate the channel is Evanston's Ladd Arboretum southwest of Green Bay Road. It is home to the Evanston Parks Ecology Center as well as a remarkable variety of plant life and more than 100 species of trees from around the world. South of the center at Bridge Street are the International Garden and the arboretum's Peace Garden.

Cuneo brownfield site on the Chicago River (Brian Loll/Chicago Department of Environment)

The channel finally reverts to a wild, natural appearance as it moves through the Peter N. Jans Community Golf Course and then past the Baha'i House of Worship toward its outlet at Wilmette Harbor.

The South Branch

When the first settlers arrived, the South Branch had two major forks. The west one meandered off toward the Des Plaines River, traversing on its way a shallow, miserable body of water known as Mud Lake. The South Fork, known as Bubbly Creek, led nowhere except into the prairie.

The West Fork and Mud Lake served Native Americans and fur traders as an all-important portage route to the Des Plaines, Illinois and Mississippi rivers. Later, it provided the beginning stretch of the Illinois and Michigan Canal and, starting in 1900, the Chicago Sanitary and Ship Canal.

During the 1800s and early 1900s, Bubbly Creek (east of Ashland Avenue and today just a stub of a creek) served a less reputable function. It was the sewer for the Union Stockyards, located on the Near Southwest Side of the city.

WHO'S DOING WHAT?

The Chicago Department of Environment and the United States Corps of Engineers have joined forces in a "River Partnership" to improve the aesthetics and ecological health of the river.

Planning assistance has come from Friends of the Chicago River, the Chicago Department of Planning and Development, and the Metropolitan Water Reclamation District.

Their initial plans (for Spring 2001) included the restoration of four Chicago riverbank sites through bank stabilization.

The following work has also been scheduled or completed:

South Branch

- Cuneo site (500 block of West Cermak Road). Fish shelters installed underwater to improve their aquatic habitats.
- The banks are being "naturalized" by planting vegetation along their slopes.

North Branch

- Weed Street (1550 North). A new canoe launch is being created to provide greater recreational access to the river.
- Von Steuben High School (5000 block of North Kimball Avenue). Lab classes are scheduled to be held on the riverbank, native plantings are being made to create a new habitat and a structure is being added to provide public access via canoes and kayaks.

North Shore Channel

- North Side College Prep High School (5500 block of North Kedzie Avenue). The same program has been set up as at Von Steuben High School.

The South Branch, like the rest of the river system, has come a long way and undergone significant changes since the days of the Indians' canoes, the fur traders' *bateaux* and the early canal boats, or even since the days of the stockyards. Indeed, its direction has had to be reversed twice since the days when it carried the yards' waste out into Lake Michigan.

Even within the last decade or so, there have been major changes. What figure from the past could have fathomed that there would be a large apartment/office complex known as River City along it?

Even more amazing to someone from the past might be the small, new park built on the bank of the South Branch in 1999 at 300 West Nineteenth Street. Known as Ping Tom Memorial Park, it is strictly Chicago Chinese. Its design complements the adjacent Chinatown neighborhood in architecture, color and plant life.

The attractive little area has a pagoda covered with red and orange tiles, four matching columns and a bright dragon. Plants scattered throughout it are ones a visitor would expect to find in a park in China.

The park has a state-of-the-art children's playground, complete with poured-in, rubberized surfaces.

Across the river, on the north bank, are short canals and boat slips. When summer is over, these store large numbers of Lake Michigan's yachts and sailboats.

Underwater shelters have been created along the banks to make the South Branch more fish-friendly. Other improvements include elimination of many eyesores such as railroad yards and junk fields, as well as the planting of trees, grass, shrubs and flowers along the banks.

Canoes can be rented on the river at Clark Park, just south of Addison Street in Chicago. For information, call 773-32-KAYAK. Another provider is Chicagoland Canoe Base at 4019 North Narragansett Avenue. They can be reached at 773-777-1489.

3. The Sistine Chapel in an OAK GROVE: NORTH BRANCH RESTORATIONISTS RECOVER A SAVANNA

Vestal Grove is a work in progress, its unfolding controlled by nature's hazily understood laws of ecosystem assembly. But if the North Branch restorationists succeed, they will have restarted a natural process that enables as many species as possible not to die, but to survive, evolve and to adjust to a landscape drastically altered and fragmented by humans.

—WILLIAM K. STEVENS,
MIRACLE UNDER THE OAKS: THE REVIVAL OF NATURE IN AMERICA

An ecological miracle has been wrought on a small patch of land along Dundee Road in Northbrook. It has created excitement across the country, and was not only the inspiration for a *New York Times* article, but also the subject of a best-selling book.

The miraculous event was the rediscovery of a lost ecosystem, the oak savanna.

Somme Prairie, a 90-acre site adjacent to the North Branch of the Chicago River, was on a list of ten volunteer nature restoration projects in various spots along or near the river. The others included: Sedge Meadow, Watersmeet, Harms Woods, Wayside Prairie, Miami Woods Prairie, Bunker Hill Prairie, Edgebrook Flatwoods and Sauganash Prairie Grove.

A small piece of Somme Prairie called Vestal Grove received special attention. It was celebrated in a *New York Times* article by William K. Stevens and later in his book, *Miracle Under the Oaks: The Revival of Nature in America* (Pocket Books, 1995). Stevens saw what happened at

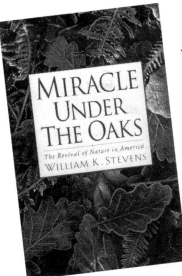

Vestal Grove as both an important discovery and a dramatic step forward in the grassroots movement to revive nature in America.

Writing in the premiere (Fall 1997) issue of *Chicago Wilderness,* Sheryl De Vore also repeated the story of Vestal Grove, calling its restoration the "ongoing rescue of a vital link in this region's chain of existence."

This was more than the finding of a plant or animal previously unknown or believed to be extinct; it was the recovery of an entire, significant habitat. It signaled an unexpected first strike against the large-scale destruction of natural ecosystems in the nation and especially in the Midwest.

Stevens' book called the North Branch Prairie Project Restorations site "the flagship of an enterprise in which, as of 1993, more than 3,000 volunteers were restoring 17,000 acres of the prairie-savanna mosaic on 142 sites in the Chicago area."

When Steve Packard, a conservation biologist with the Nature Conservancy, found the Vestal Grove site in the mid-1970s, he realized this natural habitat was on the edge of oblivion.

The words of *Miracle Under the Oaks* echoed Packard's perception, describing the habitat there as: "not just dead, but lost to human ken. The classic tallgrass savannas had disappeared so quickly, before scientists could study them, that their ecological characteristics were almost unknown."

This grove had been invaded and choked by 20-foot-high thickets of European buckthorn. The site was strewn "with mattresses, car seats and milk crates that teenagers used as seats for outdoor parties. Kentucky Fried Chicken take-out cartons, plastic buckets and an automobile muffler decorated the ground."

Starting in 1977, Packard and a group of volunteers began clearing the land and restoring what they felt had been there originally, a prairie. They studied and followed all the known rules to do so, but their basic assumption proved wrong. It was not a prairie. The flora and fauna they had painstakingly planted did not take to the site, and members of the group became deeply frustrated. Packard finally chose to change course and restore the land based not on the tallgrass blueprint, but on a different vision of nature—the oak savanna.

Packard did not know exactly what an oak savanna was. No one did. A list of appropriate plants had to be culled from old historical documents describing the area and from oak-dominated patches of land along railroad tracks, in vacant lots and in cemeteries.

The oak trees were the key.

The biologist and his associates took seeds from plants growing in open spots around oak trees and brought them to Vestal Grove. They reassembled an ecosystem that had barely survived in scattered pockets on the plot of land they were restoring.

The plants prospered mightily and the site became a natural habitat distinct from prairie and woods, a vibrant reality of its own.

Astoundingly, at the same time, Wayne Lampa of the Lake County Forest Preserve District and Gerould Wilhelm of the Morton Arboretum discovered a different path to restoring oak savannas. They started burning and cutting brush in the oak woods at Waterfall Glen in Lake County Forest Preserves. Miraculously, an oak savanna—a unique selection of plant life—arose from the ashes on the seemingly barren land.

"Every time I walk through [Vestal Grove] I get all tingly," Packard told the *New York Times* writer. "I feel this great excitement and peace at the same time, the way you might feel walking into the Sistine Chapel. It's almost holy. It's rich, healthy and ancient—and young at the same time."

WHAT ARE OAK SAVANNAS?

Oak savannas are generally flat, open areas. They have oak trees, but are clear enough that a person on a horse could easily ride through them. For this reason they were once called "openings."

They are half prairie and half oak forest, but support a different variety of plants than either of these ecosystems. Only an expert, however, can make a clear distinction.

THE WONDERS OF THE NEWLY DISCOVERED HABITAT

The finely tuned ecosystems of Vestal Grove, Waterfall Glen and other oak savannas now blaze with the colors of such plants as false dragonhead, rattlesnake master, cream gentian, mad-dog skullcap, swamp buttercup, maple-leafed goosefoot and bloodroot.

Located along the north side of Dundee Road just west of Waukegan Road, Vestal Grove has become the model for restoring other oak savanna sites throughout the area.

Packard, Lampa, Wilhelm and their associates made a recovery rather than a discovery. Theirs proved a significant step in an ongoing effort by more than ten thousand volunteers, who are working to restore more than 100,000 acres of primeval habitat—prairies, savannas and woods—in the Chicago area.

■ 4. Lake MICHIGAN I:
EVER BEAUTIFUL AND STILL FREE

Lake Michigan exerts an irresistible pull. What's out there? It has faraway places, unseen distant shores, and shimmering islands floating on the horizon. Humans flock to the water's edge and look into the vastness; sooner or later, nearly all of us lean down and touch the water. This simple ritual brings us closer to the lake's wild essence.

—JOHN AND ANN MAHAN, *WILD LAKE MICHIGAN*

Lake Michigan can be fabulous (on any given day), friendly (most of the time) and free (at least in Chicago.)

Chicago's lake is not a mere thing of beauty, but rather something with which people can have a relationship. It can feel like a warm spring breeze or a frigid winter's blast. How deeply it can touch a soul the way a close friend can, or disturb one's calm like a raging thunderstorm!

As the twenty-first century unfolds, the lake increasingly seems to embody change, enhancement, restoration and renewal.

Where there were rocks, there will be beaches; where there was cement, grass; where there was pollution, oxygen-exhaling trees; where people feared to tread, strollers.

The most dramatic changes are taking place on the shoreline, specifically Burnham Park, the stretch of beach from south of the Museum Campus to Jackson Park and the Museum of Science and Industry.

Aerial view of the North Side lakeshore (City of Chicago/Peter J. Schulz)

THE NEW SPLENDOR OF CHICAGO

Other improvements have been made or are being made on the lake's shoreline to the north and along Grant Park.

Chicagoans recognize the importance of these changes as their vision broadens and they increasingly embrace the lake as ripe with possibility and rich with beauty.

The Lake's Beaches

> *There live not any happier group of mortals than the crowd that swarms the Chicago beaches of Lake Michigan in summer, even within the shadow of the Loop.*
>
> —WEIMAR PORT

Chicago has been long noted for its many miles of free and handsome beaches. These serve all as places of rest and activity, where sun, sand and lake together dance the dance and sing the song.

FROM THE ANNUAL REPORT 2000 OF THE LAKE MICHIGAN FEDERATION

We all have our transcendent moments at the lake. For one of our board members, it's "saying hello to the lake" as he stands at the front of the No. 6 bus on his way to work. For me, one moment is the trek with my teenage son to watch the waves crash over the Belmont Harbor rocks in the wildest storms.

Many of our members have their moments as avid sailors, away from shore. Those who live near the dunes have a totally different panorama of pastel hues, for example. Such is the lake's vastness that we can enjoy the familiar pleasures and still keep being surprised by new wonders.

The Lake Michigan Federation has an energetic staff, committed volunteers, dedicated board and a healthy outlook. All are crucial ingredients to do good work, as Lake Michigan remains under the pall of past excesses: continuing land abuse, industrial contamination and insufficient fish and wildlife habitats. At the same time, more people are enjoying Lake Michigan. Let us work harder, together—having fun along the way—to each do our small part to preserve those opportunities for transcendent moments.

—ELLEN PARTRIDGE, PRESIDENT

Postcard view of swimmers in pre–World War I Chicago

These easily accessible beaches have a special beauty, one which is anything but passive, but rather active and eager. Here, families with small children hunch up against the shoreline to invite the anxious waters to come and fill gouged-out basins of sand or wear away ephemeral castles and the tiniest of temporary mountains.

The wearing away of the sand beach itself, however, is the greatest threat to Chicago's beaches. At last, authorities are dealing with this problem through *revetments,* cement steps extending out into the lake.

Pollution is the other major issue facing the beaches of Chicago. It is sometimes created by stormy weather stirring up past pollutants that lie on the bottom of Lake Michigan. At other times, it comes from heavy rains and flooding that result in the North Channel dumping them into the lake.

The area's Deep Tunnel Project hopefully will address these problems, both now and for the future. The multi-million-dollar project will carry in its underground tunnels the tainted waters that would otherwise have been loosed on the lake.

The beaches also acquire pollution from other sources. In 1999, Chicago's 63rd Street Beach was closed more than 20 times because of high bacteria counts. The problem was eventually traced to a broken sewer pipe that doesn't even come close to the lake.

The Lake Michigan Federation, horrified by the problem, called upon lakeside communities to inventory their sewer infrastructures and put together plans to upgrade them so as to avoid future beach pollution.

Chicago's Lakefront Water Trail

> *Looking north, I saw the whitewashed buildings of Fort Dearborn sparkling in the sunshine, our boats with flags flying, and our oars keeping time to the cheering boat song. I was spellbound and amazed at the beautiful scene before me.*
>
> —GURDON SALTONSTALL HUBBARD,
> ARRIVING AT CHICAGO BY CANOE IN 1818

Of all the free brochures and pamphlets offered by Chicago area organizations and agencies, perhaps the most interesting and surprising is the Chicago Park District's map of the new lakefront water trail.

People with a love of the lake and an empty wall might want to get a copy and post it there. The brochure is only 3 1/2 inches square, but folds out to 21 inches in length and offers a use for the lake few Chicagoans have ever contemplated—as a canoe trail.

The map represents almost 24 miles of lakefront from one end of the city to the other. On the shore, it offers details for 18 miles of running, walking, biking and in-line skating paths along with symbols for water fountains, park facilities and mileage markers.

Out in the water is the surprise. A line parallel to the shore marks a water trail for "canoes, kayaks and other, small human-powered boats."

Along the shore are 11 periodically spaced launch/land sites. These, from north to south, are:

- Leone Beach
- Wilson Launch Ramp
- Montrose Beach
- Montrose Harbor
- Diversey Harbor North
- Diversey Harbor South
- 12th Street Beach
- 31st Street Beach
- 63rd Street Beach
- Rainbow Beach
- Calumet Launch Ramp.

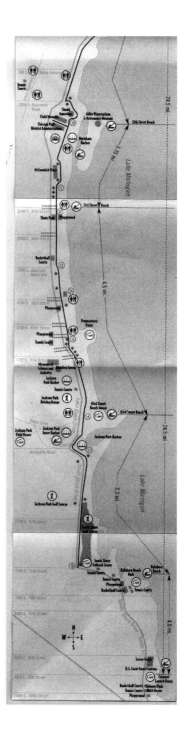

The brochure cautions:

When using the water trail, please remember:

1. Paddling on the lake is recommended for experienced, well-equipped paddlers. Less experienced paddlers should be accompanied by an experienced group or guide.
2. Always wear a personal flotation device (PFD).
3. Be able to communicate. Carry a whistle, flare, cell phone or radio to signal for help. Dial 911 or reach Channel #16 Marine FM in an emergency.
4. Be visible. Display a white light at night.
5. Pick up. Keep the lakefront clean by placing litter in the proper receptacle after your visit.

Even though a person might never canoe or kayak Lake Michigan, this trail represents a dream, a reminder of a new possibility for adventure.

5. Lake MICHIGAN II:
FROM CHALLENGE TO CHANGE

With 24 miles and 2,990 acres of shore parks, Chicago has the greenest, most accessible and most inviting lakefront in the United States.

—PETER HARNIK, *INSIDE CITY PARKS*

Chicago has long been proud and boastful of its incredible lakefront, but in 1997 a *Chicago Tribune* series by Blair Kamin reminded the city that the lakeshore needed to be "reinvented." The articles would be awarded the 1998 Pulitzer Prize for criticism.

In the first article in the series, Kamin wrote:

> The lakefront is Chicago's undisputed jewel, a timeless treasure that brings dazzling images to mind: of fireworks and bandshells, sailboats dotting blue waters, museums rising like wedding cake from a sweeping expanse of green, skyscrapers winking in the night sky. Our front yard, the lakeshore, is the face Chicago presents to the world.

> But zoom in on the 30-mile stretch of beaches, harbors and parkland between Indiana and Evanston and troubling blemishes appear. What you see is a resource that is in serious imbalance, alternately overwhelmed and underachieving, a carelessly treated beauty that has lost much of its sheen.

If his meaning were not completely clear to all, here are some comments from a subsequent article in the series:

> Nothing is more shameful about Chicago's lakefront than the fact that it is really two lakefronts—one for those who are black and poor, and another for everybody else.

> Nothing is more important to the lakefront's future—and perhaps the city's—than redressing this historic imbalance.

His commentary reflected the long-unheeded complaints of the South Side poor and African-Americans, who would have benefited from an equal development of public parkland up and down the lakefront.

The *Tribune* series argued that Burnham Park, just to the south of the Loop area from Roosevelt Road to 56th Street, had long suffered from

THE 1919 WAR FOR THE LAKEFRONT

In 1919, the city went to war with itself, white against black, over whose beaches Chicago's were. A group of whites refused to let a young African-American teenager swim in from deep water to "their" beach. They threw stones and he drowned as a result. Chicago flared into a major, bloody race riot over the act. Afterwards, a "Blue Ribbon" commission representing the establishment decreed that the solution was to keep African-Americans even more segregated to prevent such an incident from happening again in Chicago.

REVETMENTS: STEPS OUT INTO THE LAKE

As the twentieth century ended, engineers realized that Chicago's shoreline was in serious trouble. The year-by-year erosion and the powerful thrusts of lake waves had taken a heavy toll over the years. The effectiveness of the cement and stone structures erected between 1910 and 1931 to protect the shore from flood and storm damage had crumbled away almost completely.

The U.S. Corps of Engineers estimated that eight miles of Chicago's shoreline, including sections from Montrose Harbor south to 57th Street, needed to have new devices constructed to save the lakefront, its beaches, parks and famed Lake Shore Drive.

In their labs, the Corps' technicians were able to simulate storm conditions. They tested the impact on 18 shoreline models of different shapes and sizes to learn which one could best buffer the hard driven waves. The ultimate solution on which they settled is a series of revetments, or cement steps, extending out into the lake. Constructing these would protect the shoreline in key places against both persistent erosion and future storm damage.

To do so, however, would take seven years and cost $300 million.

All funding would come jointly from the City of Chicago, the State of Illinois and the federal government. The Corps of Engineers would be in charge of the work and would also refurbish the beaches along the stretch with new sand.

"benign neglect." Most people were not even certain that this stretch of lakefront actually was a park.

Despite the Kamin articles and the prestigious journalism award it received, few Chicagoans believed the city would ever do anything about the situation, much less attempt to change it substantially.

Former Lake Michigan Federation director Lee Botts had said, "The people and powers that be in Chicago . . . have continued to brag about (the lakefront), tout its virtues and its values to the city while they continue to let it fall apart."

Six months after the series ran, however, city, state and federal officials committed themselves to an ambitious plan and joint funding to redevelop the South Side Burnham Park completely by 2010.

Within a year, the three levels of government announced an additional $300 million program to restore eight miles of beach and lakefront, including Burnham Park, using what are called *revetments*. Spokesmen predicted the work would make such substantial shoreline improvements that it could help advance Burnham Park's completion deadline from 2010 to 2005.

With the revetment plan as an integral first step, Chicago was committed to a major transformation for Burnham Park. There were great concerns about how to do it. The planners sought community input, but they also looked back almost 130 years, as many of their "new" ideas turned out to be the same as those first outlined for the beautification of the Chicago lakefront by Frederick Law Olmsted and his partner Calvert Vaux in 1871.

In a letter to the South Park Commissioners, the two men presented a specific vision for a lakefront park in what was then the Chicago suburb of Hyde Park. The letter was written six months before the Chicago Fire of 1871.

Their proposal was to create a 1,000-acre South Park. Even though their plans were burned in the Chicago Fire, the large park was eventually created and today includes Jackson Park, Washington Park and the Midway Plaisance, a corridor connecting the two.

Olmsted and Vaux wanted to serve Chicagoans far into the future and their plans have done just that. One hundred thirty years after the proposal was written, lakefront critics reread their letter and used it to suggest how Burnham Park could best be upgraded.

Here are some of the phrases and ideas from the 1871 Olmsted and Vaux letter and parallels from the plans for Burnham Park.

Olmsted & Vaux   "There is but one object of scenery near Chicago of special grandeur or sublimity, and that [is] the lake."

Burnham Park   The lake is the focus of the park concept. The district's ambitious but flexible plans were written to enhance

---

ROBERT LAW OLMSTED AND CALVERT VAUX

These two men designed not only Jackson and Washington parks in Chicago but also Central Park in New York, Fenway Park in Boston, Belle Isle in Detroit and the Chicago suburb of Riverside.

Their ideas worked so well that in his recent book *Inside City Parks,* Peter Harnik praised Chicago's Jackson Park, describing it as "an Olmstedian landscape that seems to make the city disappear."

	the lakeshore beaches, greenway, paths and facilities from Meigs Field to Jackson Park.
Olmsted & Vaux	The "present duty [of the park] is first of all to the whole city."
Burnham Park	The park development was designed to serve all Chicago, especially the part of the whole which had been ignored until now.
Olmsted & Vaux	"The first obvious defect of the site is that of its flatness . . . . It must be overcome, at any cost, by artificial elevations and depressions."
Burnham Park	Landscaping calls for trees, dunes, hills, ponds, wetlands and a nature garden.
Olmsted & Vaux	The park "should be adapted to the convenient movement of a large number of people pursuing recreation in a variety of ways."
Burnham Park	One of the earliest additions to Burnham Park was a skate park, the first in the city of Chicago. Other additions include facilities for all ages and interests: beaches, deep water swimming lanes, playgrounds, a fishing pier, a cycling and strolling path, an in-line skating and ice rink, tennis courts, a picnic area, a great lawn, an overlook and a beach building with concessions and multi-purpose rooms.
Olmsted & Vaux	"Searching for a natural type of what is thus desirable, we look first for local suggestions."
Burnham Park	Several well-publicized community meetings were held to allow citizens to add local input.
Olmsted & Vaux	"Accessibility from the heart of the city by water passage."
Burnham Park	Burnham Park will include canoe and kayak access.

Olmsted & Vaux	"It may have a beauty and an interest of its own, in which the citizens of Chicago for generations to come shall take a just pride, and all the more so that it has been the result of their fathers' pride upon a sandbar."
Burnham Park	The ambitious plans for the park are about the future, starting with the substantial work and funds being invested in the revetments. The redesigning of the area will continue to benefit Chicagoans "for generations to come."
Olmsted & Vaux	"The beach [is to be] guarded against the drift of sand by a pier . . . as near to the heart of the park as possible."
Burnham Park	The newly constructed revetments guard against the drift of sand. Still to be added, however, are a pier and more sand for the beaches.
Olmsted & Vaux	"There should be enough 'open' ground at least for local use, night and day, near each of the extreme parts of your plan."
Burnham Park	Considerable "open ground" will be added to the park through lakefill, creating a great lawn, several large picnic areas and an impressive greenway the length of the park.
Olmsted & Vaux	The plan "offers to those coming by rail, in public carriages or on foot, a means of traveling through nearly all the parts of the park, quietly, agreeably and

PAST BATTLES TO SAVE THE LAKEFRONT

Evanston once attempted to protect its lakefront with whatever buffers the city could find, including a pile of old tombstones. They are still there.

In the early 1950s, lakeside mansions and homes along the Wisconsin-Illinois border in Edithton Beach, Wisconsin, and Winthrop Harbor, Illinois, fought the battle and lost. Lake Michigan eventually claimed every house except one whose owner threw everything but his kitchen sink into the lake to save his home. The house is now on the small man-made peninsula he built up.

THE NEW SPLENDOR OF CHICAGO

without fatigue, and by a method much less expensive than that of wheeled carriages. This will be of great value to invalids, convalescents and mothers with children in arms."

Burnham Park   The wide pathway for hiking and cycling will extend the length of the park. A major consideration during the Burnham Park renovations was accessibility, because South Lake Shore Drive cuts the park off from the city. The plans call for plenty of parking, the development of the bike path, bus routes stops at several sites within the park, and seven bridges across or tunnels under the Drive.

The Chicago Park District has indeed wrought what Olmsted and Vaux envisioned.

16. Millennium Park ALIVE:
SURROUND SOUND
FOR THE OUTDOORS

This is a gift for the next century.

—MAYOR RICHARD M. DALEY, 1999

Millennium Park, located in the northeast quadrant of Grant Park, is Chicago's new center for free musical and theatrical celebration. It will reverberate in the summers of the twenty-first century with a sound fidelity that should please even the most demanding of musicians.

Prior Grant Park music shells have afforded the city its summer classical and popular concerts under the stars, free Fourth of July Chicago Symphony concerts, the annual Chicago Summer Dance Festivals and many other music fests. This new stage, however, is bigger, more ambitious and of far greater beauty in landscaping and design than anything that preceded it.

The critics, in giving this park-within-a-park a thumbs-up, describe it as special in concept, execution and promise. They add that its world-famous architect, Frank Gehry, has outdone himself.

Constructed with an eye to the future, this public music stage and entertainment complex can accommodate a live audience of more than 10,000 and features a sound system better than any previously available.

Artist's rendering of Millennium Park (Michael McCann/ Skidmore, Owings & Merrill)

The pavilion, with fixed seating for 4,000, has an adjoining "Great Lawn" area that provides additional room for 7,000 more listeners. This area is twice as long as a football field and three times as wide.

Color plays a major role in the beauty of Millennium Park. The red-tiled trellised music pavilion with its great projections of stainless steel sits on a great green expanse of trees and grass next to a wall of majestic white and gray skyscrapers, and looks out onto the vast body of Lake Michigan's blue-green waters.

The heart of Millennium Park is the imaginatively designed and crafted Music Pavilion.

Architect Frank Gehry had designed several of the most innovative cultural facilities throughout the world, including the Guggenheim Museum

A CHOICE SITE

Situated on 24.6 acres in the northwest corner of the city's front lawn, Millennium Park is bounded by Michigan Avenue, Columbus Drive, Randolph Street and Monroe Street. Two-thirds of this area was formerly open-air right-of-way for the Illinois Central Railroad.

THE NEW SPLENDOR OF CHICAGO

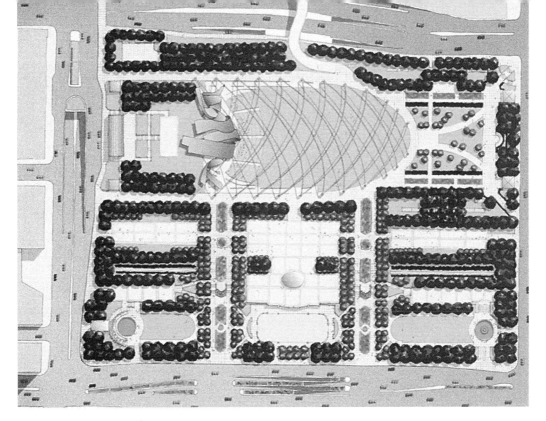

in Bilbao, Spain, and the Museum Project in Seattle. He worked with the Chicago firm of Skidmore, Owings & Merrill to create the Music Pavilion and help incorporate it into the city surrounding it.

The requirements for Gehry's design presented an incredible challenge: an outdoor music setting does not produce the "surround sound" of a music hall. Musicians want an echoing chamber rather than the great outdoors for the best projection of notes, both vocal and instrumental.

Understandably, top-flight musicians do not like to play where the sound situation is less than optimal and their skills and instruments cannot be utilized to maximum effect.

Until now, the one and only solution to this problem has been to hang multiple speakers from a large number of posts. But Mayor Daley had stated emphatically that he and Chicago did not want a forest of columns covering the Great Lawn.

PAST HONORS FOR THE ARCHITECT OF THE PARK

Frank Gehry, has been the recipient of many awards including the Royal Gold Medal for Architects, the Pritzker Prize in Architecture and the 1998 Medal of Art.

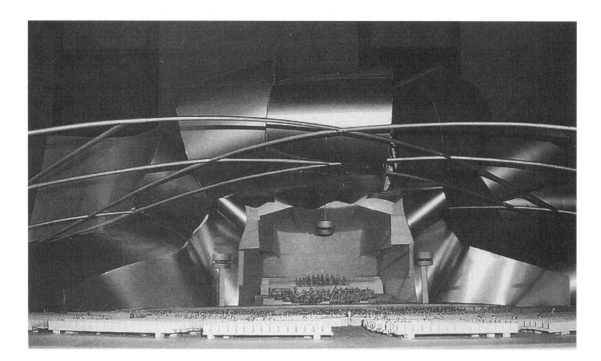

Model of Frank Gehry's bandshell, front (Skidmore, Owings & Merrill)

Instead of such poles holding the roof and the speakers, Gehry designed an arching trellis structure, which covers both the entire seating area and the Great Lawn. It is grounded only along the edges of the elliptically shaped field, where it is supported by columns. Elsewhere, it floats over the seating area.

This ingenious piece of trelliswork, which holds the speakers and lights, prevents pillars from obstructing anyone's view of the stage.

Even more importantly, the broadcast of the music is not impeded. The effect is a "surround sound" in the out of doors.

The Gehry sense of style is clearly a part of the design—huge ribbons of sculptural stainless steel curl dramatically outward and upward from the central stage.

The stage, while similar in proportion to that of Orchestra Hall, can be increased in size by means of risers, creating a three-row choral terrace for at least 150 musicians.

The Talaske Group, Inc., was asked to develop a new acoustic enhancement system for the pavilion. In response, its staff created an "equal onstage sound" along with the pavilion's special sound reinforcement system.

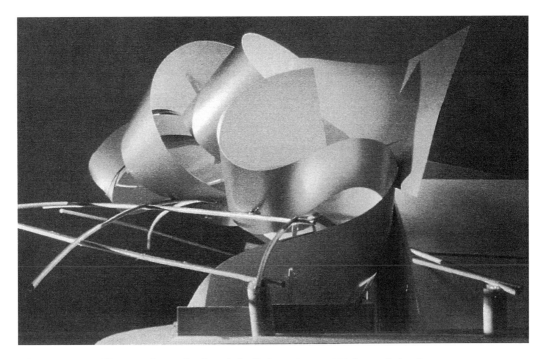

The music pavilion replaces the band shell that since 1978 hosted the free summer concerts by the Chicago Symphony Orchestra and Chorus, part of the Grant Park Music Festival program. The former structure was also center stage for innumerable summer music festivals as well as the annual, world-famous blues, jazz, Gospel and folk music fests.

Model of Frank Gehry's bandshell, side (Skidmore, Owings & Merrill)

During those years—and for 43 more before 1978, when the band shell was located three quarters of a mile south—the various Grant Park music programs were free and attended over the years by millions of Chicagoans and visitors from around the world.

Millennium Park is more than the Music Pavilion, however. It also includes:

- *The Music and Dance Theater Chicago.* This structure, back to back with the Music Pavilion, will house a number of Chicago performing arts groups as well as the much-loved Old Town School of Folk Music.

A COMING TOGETHER OF THE PEOPLE

Grant Park concerts and music fests have mingled people of all races and backgrounds: rich and poor, young and old, sophisticated music lovers and people who simply loved the park and its lack of an entrance fee.

This theater will share dressing and warm-up rooms with the Music Pavilion. Its season will run from September through May, while the Grant Park Music Festival programs will be held only during the summer months.

Many observers have short-changed Chicago's reputation in the performing arts, largely because the city's cultural scene is perceived as fragmented. By bringing together two very different arts groups, Millennium Park can help focus the parallel creative forces of Chicago.

- *The Anish Kapoor Sculpture.* Another feature of Grant Park is this large elliptical stainless steel mirror that reflects the landscape and nearby structures.

  Kapoor, a resident of Great Britain, is a native of India and has lived in Israel. He resists any attempts to characterize him as an Indian or British artist, but points rather to the universality of his work. This was his first public work ever installed in the United States.

- *The Millennium Mosaic.* At the entrance to the new park is a mosaic that represents the work not of a world-renowned artist, but rather of 5,000 amateur ones, children and adults who, in 1999, created individual tiles for the mosaic. These were composed and installed as a free-form mural at the Randolph Street entrance to the garage built underneath the park.

- *The Peristyle.* In 1953, a number of historic structures in Grant Park were demolished in order to accommodate a new underground parking garage. One was the Peristyle, a semicircular wall of Doric columns that had stood in the park since 1917. The neo-classical structure was designed by Edward Bennett, Daniel Burnham's co-author on *The Plan of Chicago.*

Now the Peristyle has been recreated in the northwest corner of Millennium Park, in an area known as Wrigley Square. OWP&P Architects based the colonnade and the fountain they enclose on Bennett's original designs.

7. The New Museum CAMPUS:
CEMENTSCAPE TO GREENSCAPE

The Grant Park Museum Campus ... [is] architecturally the most impressive "cultural center" in the United States.

—AUTHOR AND CRITIC CARL CONDIT

At the end of the twentieth century, three world-class museums and one historic stadium underwent a dramatic reorganization. These cultural institutions, located off the southeast corner of Grant Park, had long been separated by parking lots, Lakeshore Drive and other cement-covered spaces. Now, they sit together within one vast park, the cement and asphalt replaced by greenery and gardens.

This new cluster is known as the Museum Campus, and its stars are:
- The Field Museum of Natural History
- The John G. Shedd Aquarium
- The Max Adler Planetarium and Astronomical Museum
- Soldier Field

Until the Museum Campus plan was realized, the Field Museum and Soldier Field were isolated to the west of the other two institutions. They were disconnected from the planetarium and aquarium by the fast-moving lanes of South Lake Shore Drive, and surrounded by large expanses of uninviting cement. That same highway also cut them off from any free and easy access to Lake Michigan.

Flowers and greenery frame the Field Museum (John Weinstein/The Field Museum)

In 1996, work began to bring the four sites together. The multi-lane northbound traffic on Lakeshore Drive was rerouted to the west side of the Field Museum and Soldier Field, thus putting all four facilities into one grouping. Their connection, formerly a tunnel under the Drive, is now a handsome, wide walkway through an attractively landscaped park.

The regrouping has also given the City of Chicago a major opportunity to plant many additional trees and flowers, creating for Chicago and its visitors a place of great beauty.

The transformation has done more than change the appearance of this special lakefront area. It has been like making a university out of separate

THE GREENSCAPE

The Chicago landscaping firm of Teng & Associates has enhanced the area immeasurably, especially in front of the Field Museum. Trees there frame the classical structure. They give shade and a natural contrast to the white marble building. Adjoining gardens invite people to come, sit and reflect, or even have a picnic.

colleges, a tiara crown for the city out of four distinct jewels. The Museum Campus has put together an interactive ensemble of cultural sites that allows each to share in the renown of the others.

Chicago's signature—trees, flowers, statue and shoreline on the Museum Campus (Brook Collins/Chicago Park District)

Its timing proved extraordinary. One after another, in a matter of a few years, all four institutions had added spectacularly to their individual reputations.

The Field Museum

Chicago's celebrated natural history museum now has Sue, a 42-foot-tall *Tyrannosaurus Rex* skeleton. Sue is not only extraordinarily large, but is also the most complete T-Rex skeleton ever unearthed. The majestic, fearsome T-Rex is a unique link to the far distant past, a world 65 million years old.

OTHER ATTRACTIONS

Even before the arrival of Sue, the Field Museum was already home to world-class natural history collections. These include exhibits on anthropology, zoology, botany, geology and Egyptology. Its other attractions are everything from tiny mites to the stuffed remains of Bushman, Lincoln Park Zoo's famous 550-pound gorilla.

The Field Museum was founded in 1893 after the World's Columbian Exposition. For 27 years it was housed in the Jackson Park structure that had served the fair as the Palace of Fine Arts. It was subsequently named for Marshall Field, who had headed the department store that bears his name.

Sue provides an added bonus for those who view it. The skeletal dinosaur was reconstructed with care, accuracy and imagination to bring out a distinct personality, demonstrating both the ferocity of a hunter and a certain sense of curiosity.

A young woman, after whom Sue was named, discovered the bones in 1990 in the Hill Creek Formation of South Western South Dakota. They were purchased at auction with a grant from the McDonald Corporation. A copy of the skeleton is a part of an exhibit traveling to other major cities across the country.

The John G. Shedd Aquarium

In 1991, Shedd Aquarium added an Oceanarium, the world's largest indoor marine mammal pavilion. This addition doubled the size of the Shedd, already the largest indoor aquarium in the world.

THE NEW SPLENDOR OF CHICAGO

Like the Field Museum, the Shedd has one exhibit that captures the attention of visitors of all ages. Whereas the former has Sue, the latter has whales: beluga whales, including baby belugas, whose individual names the public chose. These babies are appreciated even by toddlers younger than the 6- and 7-year-olds traditionally fascinated by dinosaurs. Many of the younger children have seen the book, *Baby Beluga,* or at least heard the song by Raffi: "Baby Beluga, in the deep blue sea,/Swim so wild and you swim so free./Heaven above and the sea below,/A little white whale on the go."

A number of baby belugas have been born in the Oceanarium since the Shedd Aquarium first imported them in the mid-1990s. The challenge each time there is a birth is to see whether the baby will start nursing. Not all have survived.

Addition to the Shedd Aquarium (Architect: Lohan Associates; Photographer: Hedrich Blessing)

The Shedd Oceanarium (Architect: Lohan Associates; Photographer: Hedrich Blessing)

Whales are the largest mammals alive today, but their existence is fragile. A major effort to protect them has resulted in a great amount of affection toward them and interest in seeing them personally. This is true of scholars and other adults, as well as children.

HISTORY OF THE SHEDD

Built in 1929, the aquarium was truly the first of its kind, the one that others in this country have imitated. It was named after John G. Shedd, Marshall Field's successor as president of the department store. For its opening, 2,500,000 gallons of water were needed. The fresh water was pumped in from an intake in the lake east of the aquarium. The salt water was shipped in from Florida in 160 railroad tank cars.

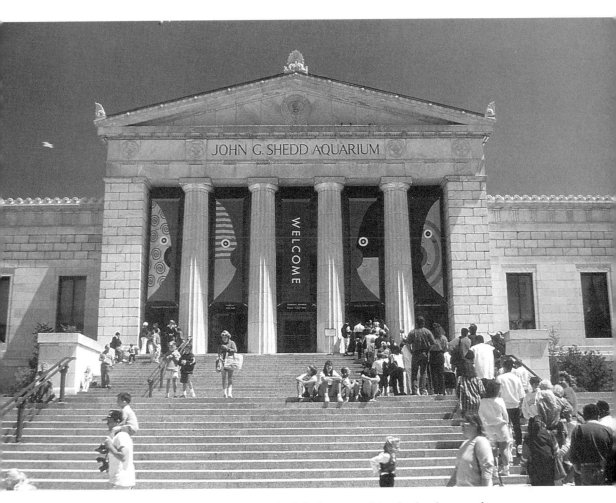

The Oceanarium was built right at the lakefront, and in the background as a person watches the whales and their keepers interacting is Lake Michigan.

John G. Shedd Aquarium (City of Chicago/Peter J. Schulz)

The Shedd has also recently renovated its Coral Reef exhibit, which features a diver hand-feeding the fish and describing the different species. Feeding hours are announced in the aquarium.

In the main building of the aquarium, an estimated 10,000 specimens represent 250 distinct species. These do not include the hatchery fish too small to exhibit. The Shedd uses six main galleries in which to exhibit its collections.

BIRTH OF THE ADLER

Max Adler, vice president of Sears, Roebuck & Company, was impressed by the Zeiss planetarium projector in Germany, and returned to Chicago to set up one of his own.

The Max Adler Planetarium

Adler Planetarium is also a proud new parent, not of adopted dinosaurs or whales, but of two innovative shows. The first of these is "Space Transporters," an exhibit that takes the visitor to Mars and beyond. The other is the Hall of Space Exploration. Futuristic special effects allow the spectator to witness the birth of a star.

The Adler boasts not only its space shows but also a collection of astronomical instruments and devices dating back centuries, with which man struggled to understand and make use of the heavens. These include instruments that predate Columbus' 1492 voyage, as well as a telescope used by Galileo.

The building is a regular dodecagon or 12-sided structure. Inset at its exterior corners are bronze plaques of the signs of the Zodiac. The sculptor lined them up in the usual counter-clockwise order.

Lohan Associates designed a new entranceway in 1981.

Soldier Field

For 75 years, this Chicago stadium has served spectators who have gathered here to watch sports, listen to concerts or attend programs ranging from political to religious.

The Chicago Park District over the years found new ways to spruce it up, alter it (even bringing in snow for a skiing event) and make it more amenable.

What was not done in those years was to make it a better neighbor, or more beautiful, more in keeping with Chicago's architectural style.

LET'S GET THE NAME RIGHT!

Many get the name of Soldier Field wrong, using an extra "'s" and calling it Soldier's Field. The stadium was renamed in 1925 by Illinois Gov. Frank O. Lowden in memory of the Americans killed in World War I and "all the fallen heroes of all wars ever fought."

Additions to Adler Planetarium (Architect: Lohan Associates; Photographer: © Steinkamp/ Ballogg, Chicago)

THE NEW MUSEUM CAMPUS: CEMENTSCAPE TO GREENSCAPE

A plan announced in November 2000 sought to correct this. The project would move the stadium's parking lot underground, replacing cement with grass and trees, an interactive fountain, a playground, walking paths and gardens.

A new, controversial "bowl" design called for $587 million of city funds, NFL loans and money made from selling fans PSLs (personal seating licenses) for approximately $2,000 each.

Critics complained that the plans were rushed through Chicago Planning Commission hearings in the spring of 2001, despite a threat by the National Park Service to strike the stadium from its list of national landmarks.

David Boland, executive director of the Landmarks Preservation Council of Illinois, said:

> We would like to express our opposition to this plan. . . . We feel that this plan, this grandstand, simply overwhelms the historic colonnade.

The Park Service requires that for a national landmark to stay on its list, any renovations to it must be "sympathetic and compatible" with the original structure. The Soldier Field plans did not meet the standard, Boland argued.

Architecturally, the stadium's Doric columns would remain out of place anywhere in the city of Chicago. So would the idea of high-priced licenses, and 133 suites for the corporate elite.

In an editorial printed on April 25, 2001, the *Chicago Tribune* was especially critical of the plan:

> The proposed design of this thing is so bizarre that even those who claim to support it must be privately embarrassed. Their plan won't just impose a vastly out-of-scale tub on what is supposed to be an attractive lakefront. It will be an international laughingstock, leaving Chicago the rube-like butt of bad-architecture jokes for decades to come. We're talking Thompson Center cubed.
>
> Maybe it's asking too much for the brokers who cut this deal to set aside their pride and stubbornness long enough to admit that they've laid an egg. That their plan will create a huge eyesore sure

to dwarf the nearby Museum Campus and even the lakefront wing of McCormick Place. And that, above all, they have traded away the memory of those who gave their lives to defend this nation for the needs of a company that owns a football team.

Soldier Field's history includes one of the most famous (or notorious) boxing matches ever, the 1927 Dempsey-Tunney "long count" heavyweight fight. In the 1920s it was also the site of International Eucharist Congress, attended by Cardinal Eugene Pacelli, later Pope Pius XII.

For many years, Soldier Field was the arena of the Football All-Star Game, which pitted the graduating all-star seniors against the National Football League champion (back when there was only one division). In recent years, it has been home for the NFL's Chicago Bears.

A few years ago, the United States hosted the World Soccer Cup championship for the first time. It was held in Soldier Field.

8. Lake CALUMET:
FROM INDUSTRIAL DECAY
TO NATURE PRESERVE

Ten years ago, there was almost no interest in doing anything at all with this area. Now, there are so many projects it is hard to keep them from overlapping.

—WALTER MARCISZ, PAST PRESIDENT, CHICAGO ORNITHOLOGICAL SOCIETY

The Lake Calumet area is being thrown enough lifelines to save the passengers and crew of the Titanic. The frightening fact is that up until a few years ago, this far South Side body of water seemed to be in almost as bad shape as the ill-fated luxury liner was after it hit the iceberg.

Chicagoans realized Lake Calumet needed saving, not only for the sake of the immediate area, but also for its extraordinary significance to the entire region. Despite being in the heart of immeasurable pollution, the Lake Calumet area has the largest collection of wetlands in the Midwest. It is also home to abundant wildlife, especially birds—its residents include the black-crowned night-heron and the yellow-headed blackbird, both on the Illinois endangered species list.

Amazingly, despite this history of pollution, the lake itself is used for fishing and has become a Mecca for anglers looking for bass.

Still, its problems date back to the 1860s, when Chicago's Union Stockyards started sending boxcars of offal there to be used by a local plant to make fertilizer. What was then the town of Hyde Park, which was along the railroad

Big Marsh, Lake Calumet region (City of Chicago)

route, had a bitter legal battle with the meatpackers and railroad for shipping the odoriferous material through it in uncovered train cars.

The lake nevertheless remained a home for sportsmen and a recreation spot for families.

George Pullman opened his Pullman Palace Car Company plant and company town next to the lake in the early 1880s, bringing industrialization to the area. He owned a five-acre island in the lake reachable by bridge and paternalistically let his employees use it for recreation on Sundays.

As a result of Pullman's high-handed dealing with his employee-tenants, they voted to incorporate the town into the City of Chicago.

Things turned really nasty for the area in 1940, when the north end of Lake Calumet was opened as a dumping site for industrial wastes. The dump has since been covered with dirt and is now a golf course.

In the late 1950s, Chicago was made an international port as part of the development of the St. Lawrence Seaway. Lake Calumet was successfully turned into a major harbor with a large enough turning basin to accommodate both ocean and lake going vessels. This brought extensive additional industrialization to the area and ever more pollution. Steel plants,

DEATH AND REBIRTH OF THE CALUMET RIVER

By the late 1800s, the Calumet had ceased to be a river and had become a series of unconnected sloughs and ponds. It was dredged in the 1870s and restored as a waterway, connecting Lake Michigan and Lake Calumet.

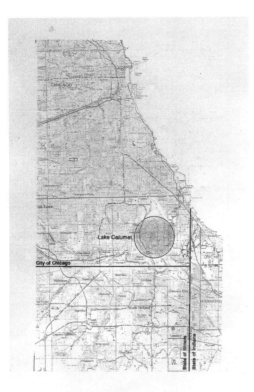

Maps shows the location of Lake Calumet (City of Chicago)

bulk storage firms, scarp yards and additional dumping sites added to the environmental woes of the area. It was here that Waste Management achieved international status amid fights with local residents and the state over pollution standards.

Yet, the birds continued to come. Wetland, marshes, prairies and a nearby pond held tenuous promise for a handful of environmentalists.

Cleansing the Calumet River

Dreams and plans abounded to restore the Calumet River, but the first action that dramatically changed things was when the Metropolitan Water Reclamation District built water-cleaning stations on the river.

River cleaning facilities called SEPA (Sidestream Elevated Pool Aeration) have been erected at five sites.

In the 1880s, the scientific community first realized that moving waters cleanse themselves, through aeration and oxygenation. They made the

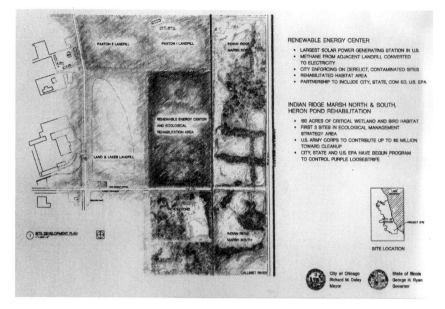

RENEWABLE ENERGY CENTER

- LARGEST SOLAR POWER GENERATING STATION IN U.S.
- METHANE FROM ADJACENT LANDFILL CONVERTED TO ELECTRICITY
- CITY ENFORCING ON DERELICT, CONTAMINATED SITES
- REHABILITATED HABITAT AREA
- PARTNERSHIP TO INCLUDE CITY, STATE, COM ED, U.S. EPA

INDIAN RIDGE MARSH NORTH & SOUTH, HERON POND REHABILITATION

- 180 ACRES OF CRITICAL WETLAND AND BIRD HABITAT
- FIRST 3 SITES IN ECOLOGICAL MANAGEMENT STRATEGY AREA
- U.S. ARMY CORPS TO CONTRIBUTE UP TO $5 MILLION TOWARD CLEANUP
- CITY, STATE AND U.S. EPA HAVE BEGUN PROGRAM TO CONTROL PURPLE LOOSESTRIFE

SITE LOCATION

City of Chicago
Richard M. Daley
Mayor

State of Illinois
George H. Ryan
Governor

Site development plan for the Lake Calumet region (City of Chicago)

discovery just in time to justify the reversal of the Chicago River. Without these cleansing processes, the river reversal would have dumped Chicago's untreated sewage on St. Louis' riverfront.

To promote oxygenation and aeration, the SEPAs pump Calumet River water into elevated pools along its bank and then let it cascade back into the stream over waterfalls. Thus, the water is purified.

The project has been so successful that the lake and river are again places not only for anglers but also for annual fishing contests.

The rehabilitation of nearby wetlands such as Dead Stick Pond, Indian Ridge Marsh North, Indian Ridge South and the Heron Pond will not be as simple as the clean-up of the river has been.

REPLACING THE RUST BELT

Industry abandoned the area in the late twentieth century, leaving behind highly polluted sites, steel housing and heavy equipment. These lands helped earn the region the nickname "Rust Belt." The government has sued to get a large number of these locations cleaned up and now is encouraging industries less damaging to the environment to find a home alongside the birds in the Calumet area.

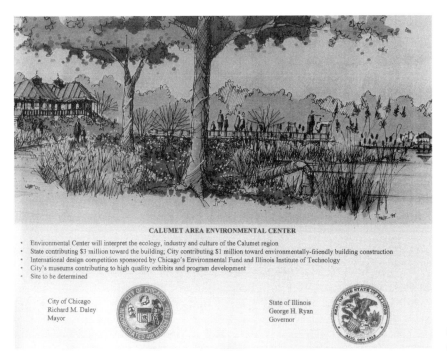

CALUMET AREA ENVIRONMENTAL CENTER

- Environmental Center will interpret the ecology, industry and culture of the Calumet region
- State contributing $3 million toward the building; City contributing $1 million toward environmentally-friendly building construction
- International design competition sponsored by Chicago's Environmental Fund and Illinois Institute of Technology
- City's museums contributing to high quality exhibits and program development
- Site to be determined

City of Chicago
Richard M. Daley
Mayor

State of Illinois
George H. Ryan
Governor

Rendering of the environmental center (City of Chicago)

In June 2000, the State of Illinois and the City of Chicago reached out with a $34 million rescue plan to create the Calumet Open Space Reserve.

The key element of this ambitious plan will be to acquire, restore and preserve available open space. The Illinois Open Land Trust quickly began the land acquisition, hoping eventually to add 1,081 acres to the 1,463 already in public hands. This space will be cooperatively managed to improve water quality and habitats as a part of a new ecological management strategy.

In addition, the state and city set out to build a renewable energy center for the Calumet area. They intend to create the largest solar power generating station in the nation. A parallel program calls for a plant to convert methane gas from landfills into electricity.

THE CALUMET AREA ENVIRONMENTAL CENTER

One of the most significant developments for the region, an environmental center, will represent the new focus on Lake Calumet and its enhancement. Specifically, the center will interpret the ecology, industry and culture of the area around the lake. It is to be a joint state- and city-funded venture. The builders are pledged to use environmentally friendly construction methods while the city's museums are to contribute to managing it and developing high quality exhibits for it.

These plans did not drop down out of the air. Throughout the 1990s, an intense effort by a long list of Chicago area environmental organizations focused on Lake Calumet and contributed valuable advice. They urged the government to buy up the land and care for it. They knew the Lake Calumet region was the worst thing happening in the area and they were determined to reverse the damage and pollution there.

The return of industry to the area, which was planned to coincide with and exist alongside the region's natural restoration, received a major boost in September 2000. Ford Motor Co. announced that it would double the size of its plant adjacent to Lake Calumet and bring 1,000 much-needed jobs back to the neighborhood.

Not many people outside of Chicago have heard of Lake Calumet or are aware that the city even has such a large body of water within its limits. In the last half century, it has not been a place of which to be proud. The future, however, is beginning to show a whole new promise.

9. Navy PIER:
A SYMBOL OF THE MARRIAGE
OF THE CITY AND THE LAKE

Today, the pier is being useful again as a cargo terminal for lake shipping. But its glory days seem gone forever.

—1968 *CHICAGO'S AMERICAN* NEWSPAPER ARTICLE

Almost ten million visitors a year aren't wrong. Navy Pier is special. It is a stroll deep into the realm of Lake Michigan amid a wide variety of twenty-first century attractions and superlative views of the city's skyline.

Over its long history, however, Navy Pier has had its ups and downs. Until the last few years, it has not come anywhere near to attaining its potential.

When it opened in 1916, Navy Pier was called Municipal Pier. After the end of World War I, Chicago's 3,000-foot extension out into Lake Michigan was renamed to honor the sailors who had lost their lives in the conflict.

For decades, Navy Pier served as port for a vast array of passenger ships, which regularly sailed across the lake to resort areas in Michigan and Indiana.

Cooled in summer by lake breezes, it became a playground for people of all ages, with amusement rides and other forms of entertainment. It hosted a beer garden, innumerable pageants and fairs, a World War II

ENTRANCE TO MUNICIPAL PIER, CHICAGO

Postcard view of Municipal Pier, now Navy Pier, prior to World War I

naval training station, a college campus (the University of Illinois at Chicago), an exposition center and a series of ethnic fairs.

In 1976, the dismally underused pier finally saw a major renovation effort with the restoration of the domed ballroom at the end of the pier. The large semi-circular area was used for dances, book fairs, Native American powwows and musical events.

In 1994, the city made a new commitment to the pier with a far more complete transformation, adding amusement rides, boat trips, restaurants and shops. It was a transformation process that still continues.

Soon the new Navy Pier was welcoming millions of visitors each summer. Many of them would choose it as the most beautiful spot in Chicago, because of its stunning views of the lake and the skyline.

Many visitors are surprised by the charming beauty of the lake and its boats as they watch a freighter cutting a straight line in the distance, a sailboat tacking, a speedboat jumping the waves or a four-masted schooner gliding alongside the pier.

The pier itself became a promenade for people to stroll, cycle or skate. Visitors pass attractions that include a 15-story Ferris wheel, a carousel, a Shakespearean theater, museums, live entertainment, concerts, a collection of imaginative public sculpture, and most recently, a new boat harbor.

THE NEW SPLENDOR OF CHICAGO

The pier is now also home for Chicago public radio station WBEZ, a lively and respected source of news, jazz, commentary and informational programming.

At the end of 2000, it hosted the world's largest-ever display of dinosaur relics.

Another highlight of Navy Pier is the wondrous Chicago Children's Museum. Located at the near end of the pier, the museum affords three floors of what it calls "kiddom." Children gather about on the pier, giggling, shouting, running and leading their parents to their next discovery.

Near to the Children's Museum is one of the pier's most popular attractions, the IMAX Theater, which seats 440 people. It boasts a 6-story–high, 80-foot–wide screen with 3D capabilities.

On the second floor pavilion is a stage whose backdrop is the city skyline. Those who entertain here include top national performers of dance, theater, blues, jazz and rock 'n' roll.

Year by year, new features have been added to enhance the reputation of Navy Pier. Here are some of the more recent additions:

- *The Pier Walk of Public Sculptures,* presented each year by the not-for-profit group 3D Chicago. The pieces are on pedestals near the far end of the pier.

  These often-stunning works of art are created by top sculptors from the around the world. Among the featured artists of past years were Sir Anthony Caro from England, Eduardo Chillida from Spain and Beverly Pepper from New York. In 2000, the walk featured several of the last pieces by the late Alexander Lieberman.

TWO FERRIS WHEELS, A CENTURY APART

The most notable feature of Navy Pier, at least from a distance, is its Ferris wheel. It is a reminder that Chicago was the site of the very first such attraction, which was a part of the World's Columbian Exposition in 1893. Attendance at the fair, it is said, had been disappointing until the day the Ferris wheel was finally completed. When it was, the number of people flocking to the fair from across the country and around the world increased dramatically.

- ***The Smith Museum of Stained Glass Windows at Navy Pier,*** dedicated solely to stained glass windows, is the first such museum in the United States. Its 800-foot–long series of galleries along the lower level terraces of Navy Pier's Festival Hall displays 150 works.

The extraordinary windows, both religious and secular, are divided into four artistic themes: Victorian, Prairie, Modern and Contemporary. Approximately 80 percent of them were installed originally in Chicago-area residential, commercial and religious buildings.

Artists represented include Frank Lloyd Wright, Louis Sullivan, Louis Comfort Tiffany and John LaFarge. The exhibit also includes lesser-known artists from stained glass studios with little public exposure.

TWO WINDOWS TO THE PAST.

Two of the more outstanding examples of windows in the museum are the Chicago Stock Exchange Ceiling Panel designed in 1894 by Louis Sullivan and the Avery Coonley Pool House Window, created by Frank Lloyd Wright.

The focus of the museum is Chicago's cultural, ethnic and religious past. The residential and commercial windows reveal the changes in architecture and decorative art styles over the last one and a third centuries.

- *The Chicago Shakespeare Theater,* a courtyard-style theater, seats 525. Its season runs from June through the end of August, and in 2000 it began offering an off-season schedule.

  Recent performances have included a 75-minute "Short Shakespeare" production of Romeo and Juliet, a Second City spoof called *Hamlet: The Musical* and Andrew Lloyd Webber's pop musical Jo*seph and the Amazing Technicolor Dream Coat.*

The Beauty of the
CHICAGO *Wilderness*

10. Ten Stories from
CHICAGO WILDERNESS:
NATURE AT YOUR NEWSSTAND

"This was not a commercial launch, but rather a mission-driven magazine. Lo and behold we found that many people are hungry for news and information about nature."

—DEBRA SHORE, EDITOR, *CHICAGO WILDERNESS*

Most of us, at one time or another, have been part of a project that should have succeeded. We wanted it to. It should have. We worked, but it didn't.

"Timing," we say afterwards.

Chicago Wilderness, a well-written and -edited quarterly publication, deals with nature in the region. It should not have worked. It was too ambitious and there seemed little reason to believe public interest was great enough.

It is succeeding.

Twenty years or even a decade ago, newspaper and magazine editors could scarcely find room for an occasional article on the subject of nature, especially in the Chicago area. The publications that existed about birds, the environment, prairies, habitats and trees were restricted to bulletins and newsletters.

Now, however, on newsstands alongside *Chicago Magazine, Crain's Chicago Business, The Chicago Lawyer, Chicago Sports* and *Chicago Bride* sits *Chicago Wilderness,* a magazine whose respect and popularity grows issue by issue.

WHAT IS CHICAGO WILDERNESS?

Here is a description from the 1997 premiere issue of the magazine bearing that name:

First and foremost, Chicago Wilderness is an archipelago of 200,000 acres of protected natural lands stretching from Chiwaukee Prairie in Wisconsin, through the six counties of northeastern Illinois and Goose Lake southwest of Joliet, to the dunes of northwestern Indiana.

Yet Chicago Wilderness is not merely land. It is the plants and animals that live on the land, the blue-spotted salamander and red-shouldered hawk, the prairie white-fringed orchid and the Hines emerald dragonfly. And the people. Native Americans were part of the wilderness here, and you and I are part of it now. Or we can be. The rich lands that comprise Chicago Wilderness are here because people saved them from the plow and pavement. . . .

Someday—for such is the goal of Chicago Wilderness—we will all recognize and cherish the fact that we also live in a land known for prairies and woods. The story of Chicago Wilderness is a tremendous American story, a story of drama, imagination and heart.

With Chicago Wilderness—*this magazine—we hope to tell that inspiring story.*

Timing and talent, a broad base of it! These factors are responsible for its success.

For generations, environmental articles with a high level of scientific inquiry have appeared only in technical magazines, where they were read at best by a few scholars. Now, equally demanding pieces are being printing on glossy paper, with color photographs and in an easily accessible writing style.

From its first issue, this magazine has occupied its own special niche.

The origin of *Chicago Wilderness* goes back to the formation in 1996 of a consortium of 34 Chicago-area conservation groups and land-owning agencies. This number has multiplied several times over since then.

The consortium chose the name Chicago Wilderness to describe itself and, almost immediately, decided to start a quarterly publication to express its reach and mission. This magazine, once launched, immediately found a receptive audience, and that audience began to grow.

The mission statement of *Chicago Wilderness* magazine is a strong one. It begins:

> Within a half hour of the nation's third largest metropolis is some of the finest and most significant nature in the temperate world, native plant and animal communities that are more rare—and their survival more threatened—than the tropical rain forests.

The magazine's stated goal is "to change the culture of the region" by "telling this inspiring story."

The magazine's creators want nothing less than to revolutionize people's lives by instilling in them a sense of appreciation for nature in the greater Chicago area. It is going to be very difficult for the populace to resist this crusade over the next few years because those who share its mission are often intense about it and their numbers are growing.

Each issue of *Chicago Wilderness* has regular features that involve the reader far more deeply than readers have come to expect from a publication on nature. The magazine profiles the dramatic effort by the area's pioneer ecologists, provides children's features, and offers interesting maps and other materials on the parks and preserves that constitute the Chicago Wilderness.

Here are synopses of the author's ten favorite articles from the early issues of this extraordinary magazine:

I. THE REBIRTH OF THE OAK WOODS

The Story of the Almost-forgotten Ecosystem Being Restored to Health

This delightfully sophisticated piece reports on the near-destruction of the oak savannas in the Chicago area. In the 1970s, several ecologists simultaneously realized that these habitats, like the tallgrass prairies, need periodic burn-offs. After a fire, the savanna begins to develop into a unique and special ecosystem, one that supports beautiful, rare plants and animal life. The article tells of the first successful efforts to restore oak woods and savannas in the Chicago area. (Fall 1997)

2. WHERE THE WILD ONES ARE

A Description of Some of the Rare Animals, Plants, Insects and Birds of the Region and Why They Are Found Here

Illinois has large concentrations of endangered species in only two areas: the Shawnee Hills in the far southern section of the state and the Chicago metropolitan area. It is in these places, for example, that one can find the rare Massasauga rattlesnake, the endangered Hines emerald dragonfly and the extremely rare lakeside daisy. (Fall 1997)

3. THE POWER OF ICE

Trekking the Glacial Landscape

This article is a field guide to help people understand the impact of glaciers on the Chicago area by exploring on foot the moraines, kettles, drifts, ridges, tills, outwashes and beaches created by the movement of these great bodies of ice. The writing here is easy to read. A *kettle*, for example, is described as "The depression left by the melting of a [giant] glacial ice cube." (Winter, 1998)

4. BIRDS AND BUILDINGS

Lethal Combo

The Field Museum's David Willard has retrieved the dead bodies of 26,000 migrating birds that crashed into one building, McCormick Place, over the last 20 years. His work and collecting have helped document important aspects of bird migration—and America's cities. "If an urban building can have the lights turned off at night, the number of birds [killed] can be reduced," Willard says. (Spring 1998)

5. GEMS OF THE BUG WORLD

Butterflies

There are approximately 100 different kinds of butterflies in the Chicago area. Since "about a third of the species are dependent on high quality natural areas," ecologists have found them to be the great barometer of ecosystem quality. (Summer 1998)

6. CITIZEN SCIENTISTS

The Amateur and the Pro

This piece points out the relationship between amateur naturalists and professional ones. This article profiles six Chicago Wilderness citizen scientists, each exploring, contributing and having a wild time, and explains: "In the young, tender world of ecosystem restoration, opportunities abound for new ideas. Indeed, yesterday's amateur scientists inspired some of the techniques used today to restore our native ecosystems." (Winter 1999)

7. MIGRATION MAGIC

Spring Birds of Chicago Wilderness

The article offers to let us "eavesdrop on a flock of veteran birders as they trade stories about the spectacular spring birds of Chicago Wilderness." One of the comments: "This was the first warbler [a black-and-white one]

I ever found on my own, as a young birder. It was an emotional thrill that I remember to this day. Everyone remembers their first warbler—you fantasize about finding them; they're so colorful and active." (Spring 1999)

8. SOGGY PLACES

The Natural History of Mucky Muck

"Soggy places" means wetlands and includes marshes, bogs, seeps and wet meadows. Some soil scientists estimate that "about half of northeastern Illinois was once sodden." The article points out that "thanks to the Clean Water Act of 1972 and to an improved understanding of the importance of wetlands, filling and draining has slowed to a trickle, so to speak," and "Children lose one of the best parts of youth when wetlands disappear from our neighborhoods." (Summer 1999)

9. LIFE UNDERGROUND

Visit a Hidden, Lively Action-packed World.
Go Underground With Us

Three quotes from this article:

1. "The world of the prairie soil is a hidden ecosystem rivaling any visible system in complexity."
2. "The real diversity of the tallgrass prairie is not above ground, but below. It is a rainforest turned upside down."
3. "The prairie soil may be one of the greatest depositories of biodiversity in the world." (Spring 1999)

10. TORKEL KORLING (1903–1998)

An American Story

This is a short biography of the late Torkel Korling, probably the most exquisite photographer ever of the plants that compose the tallgrass prairie. (The author of this book is honored to have called him a friend and to acknowledge that it was through Korling's work that he developed an interest in and appreciation for the prairie.) This article tells of his photographic technique of composing and illuminating an individual plant "up front to identify the species." The background of the photograph, meanwhile, was "filled with clouds of unfocused, but significant ecological clues: more of the same species, if their habit was to grow in masses, or a scattering of associated species that could help make clear the time and place." The *Chicago Wilderness* piece was written with the help of his wife, Diane, who worked closely with him. (Summer 2000)

11. The Birds of CHICAGOLAND:
TEN PLACES TO ENJOY THEM

*One outstanding characteristic of the birding community is that
everyone shares knowledge. I think the great beauty of our subjects, not to mention the surroundings we find ourselves in when
we are studying them, generates an enthusiasm that we just
can't keep to ourselves.*

—CAROLYN FIELDS, *CHICAGO WILDERNESS* MAGAZINE

In the twenty-first century, bird watching has become "birding," both in
the Chicago Wilderness region and throughout the country. The difference now is that participants are frequently far more than spectators who
individually enjoy the beauty of birds. Many of today's birders also count,
record, report, discuss, analyze, and, when necessary, organize and take
action to protect birds and their habitats.

The number of individuals in the area who are involved in this art, recreation and hobby has increased significantly in recent generations.

The Chicago region now boasts 12 Audubon Society chapters, the unaffil-
iated Sand Ridge Audubon Society, the Chicago Ornithological Society,
the Evanston North Shore Bird Club, the Hoy Nature Club in the Racine
and Kenosha area, and the DuPage Birding Club. These groups have a
combination membership estimated to be in excess of 10,000.

The various Chicago area bird groups and clubs have, furthermore,
formed an umbrella organization, the Bird Conservation Network. It can

Great white egret at the Lake Renwick Heron Rookery (Will County Forest Preserves)

be contacted through the Chicago Audubon Society, 5801-C North Pulaski Road, Chicago, IL 60646-6057 (773-539-6793).

The average birder has become more involved and better trained than the birdwatcher of the past.

"It gets to you," one long-time birder acknowledged. "You quickly become avid about it."

Places which people choose for birding might be one's own back yard or nearby woods and fields. Enthusiastic bird lovers learn which plants to grow in order to attract individual species such as warblers, hummingbirds, cedar waxwings or Baltimore orioles.

This region, according to many bird lovers, is one of the best places in the country to encounter a great variety of feathered residents and visitors. Because of its rivers and its proximity to Lake Michigan, the whole Chicago Wilderness is a special stopping-off place on the Mississippi River flyway, which migrating birds use to travel north and south with the seasons.

BIRDING VS. BIRD WATCHING

The transition between these two terms can be seen in an update note on a 1975 Illinois Audubon Society pamphlet titled "Bird Feeding in Illinois." The publication describes itself as "A directory of the best areas in and near the state for *bird watching*" (emphasis added). A page dated 1982 and stapled inside the front cover notes that "some information presented in this book is out of date." It then incidentally uses the term "birding areas."

THE BEAUTY OF THE CHICAGO WILDERNESS

CHICAGO'S OFFICIAL BIRD

The peregrine falcon, which nests on high cliffs near water, was elected Chicago's "official bird" on October 24, 1999. It received 39% of the vote in competition with the cedar waxwing, the common nighthawk, the eastern kingbird, the belted kingfisher and the black-crowned night-heron.

Most of the nine or so nesting pairs of peregrine falcons in Chicago live near Lake Michigan on man-made cliffs—tall buildings. Once imperiled by the pesticide DDT, the species now successfully exists even in Chicago's urban environment.

The Chicago Department of Environment, Chicago Park District, Chicago Audubon Society, Bird Conservation Network, Fort Dearborn Chapter of the Illinois Audubon Society, Chicago Ornithological and the Chicago Board of Elections jointly conducted the contest.

Like that of the mayor of Chicago, its term of office is four years.

The number of bird species that the Chicago Wilderness harbors has been estimated at around 350 and the annual number of migrating birds at 7,000,000. Here, many birds reach the northern or southern limits of their ranges. The snow goose comes from as far north as the Arctic Circle. Some birds like the plover arrive here from South America. Up to 40 species of warblers have been identified.

Birders have told of seeing such rare specimens as the ivory gull, the red-cockaded woodpecker and the pine grosbeak. Few birders have ever reported more than one sighting of these in a lifetime, however.

Some birders are able to hear promptly about recent sightings in a way they could not in the past as a result of Rare Bird Alerts (847-265-2118).

Population fluctuations are frequent. With the last two decades, several once-common species dropped as much as 90% or more in annual spring or Christmas counts. Ring-necked pheasants and purple finches are examples. Meanwhile, other species such as the double-crested cormorant are becoming more widespread than previously.

While recent habitat restorations such as that of the tallgrass prairies have helped slow the decline of some grass-dependent birds, other species will not nest in what is only a patch of prairie. They simply will not accept anything smaller than 100 or so acres.

BIRDING PLACES
IN THE CHICAGO WILDERNESS

The Chicago Wilderness offers many locally and nationally recognized birding spots. Frequently, these feature not only different habitats for birds such as herons or egrets, but also such remarkably beautiful surroundings as Lake Michigan, rivers, sloughs, historical remnants and the restored prairies.

Two new books in the field can help broaden a birder's perspective of what birding in the Chicago Wilderness is all about. They are *Birding Illinois* by Sheryl DeVore (Falcon Publishing Company, 2000) and *A Birder's Guide to the Chicago Region* by Lynne Carpenter and Joel Greenberg (Northern Illinois University Press, 1999). Both are available from the Chicago Audubon Society.

DeVore's book divides the state into five regions and lists more than 110 "premier birding locations," helping to guide the user with extensive maps. *A Birder's Guide to the Chicago Region* covers sections of Wisconsin, Indiana and Michigan as well as Illinois. It has 42 maps and describes more than 250 birding sites throughout the area.

A TREATY FOR MIGRATORY BIRDS

The treaty is an important addition to our efforts . . . to give Chicagoans the opportunity to appreciate and be stewards of the natural environment.

—MAYOR RICHARD M. DALEY

What: The signing of the Urban Conservation Treaty for Migratory Birds

When: March 25, 2000

Who: Signers were Mayor Richard M. Daley and Jamie Rappaport Clark, director of the U.S. Fish and Wildlife Service.

Why: A. To protect the 7,000,000 migratory birds that pass through Chicago annually.

        B. To enhance the quality of life for Chicago citizens and visitors.

Where: Along the shoreline, in the Loop and throughout Chicago.

How: That is the story . . .

        A. Both parties committed to a long-term relationship with $100,000 matching grants.

        B. Treaty partners will classify key habitats for migratory birds along the lakefront and in parks, cemeteries and other open spaces. They will also develop education and outreach activities to inform the public about the benefits and needs of urban and migratory birds.

        C. The city and Chicago Park District agree to enhance habitat areas for the migratory birds. They will create native landscapes that can provide food and shelter for birds. City residents will be given lists of plants that will help them create suitable backyard habitats.

        D. Homeowners will be alerted to the danger that domestic cats can cause to birds weakened by their migratory efforts.

        E. Managers of large office buildings will be encouraged to follow the John Hancock Center's example in dimming or turning out their lights at night if they are in the path of the birds.

The following is an informal list of some of the better birding locales. It comes from listening to a number of birders, talking to members of the Audubon Society and noting not only their suggestions, but also the enthusiasm with which they made them. Special help in editing the information came from the Chicago Audubon Society's Alan Anderson.

1. The Entire Palos Area

This is a suggestion that more than one birder voiced with special enthusiasm. The region is south of I-55 and west of the Tri-State 294 Tollway. It includes the Palos and the Sag Valley divisions of the Cook County Forest Preserves. These extend for seven and a half miles north and south and about three miles east and west. Consisting of 12,000 acres of forest, meadows, marshlands, lakes, sloughs, prairies and ponds, these preserves as much as any area in the region deserve to be described as "wilderness." The area affords a hilly terrain and is a place of great and varied natural beauty.

This region is special for its population of nesting warblers, which is larger than anywhere else in Cook County. Among those regularly noted have been redstart, hooded, yellow and Louisiana waterthrush warblers.

The Palos area consists of a number of distinct preserves. Many have the word "slough" as part of their names. The term refers to a shallow lake, of which there are many in the immediate area. One place for a person, especially a novice, to start birding is the Little Red School House Nature Center, at 9600 South Willow Springs Road in Willow Springs. It has two recommended paths. One is the White Oak Trail and the other goes to Long John Slough, which was named after an early Chicago mayor who owned a farm in the area.

Other Palos trails lead to sloughs with names such as Redwing, Boomerang, Katydid and Cranberry. A pair of sandhill cranes once nested in Cranberry and barred owls made a home at McClaughy Springs.

Watch for: Whip-poor-will, bald eagle, osprey and clay-colored sparrow.

2. The "Magic Hedge"

The Hedge is located at Montrose Harbor, and there is a bird sanctuary a half a mile to the south. This is the insider birding place in Chicago: if a person enjoys birding, he or she has either been here or at least heard about it. Those with a long memory in Chicago will recall that this area was the site of a controversial NIKE Missile base in the early 1960s.

Recently, organizations such as the Chicago Park District have made efforts to expand this birding area, including planting new vegetation and letting the area's existing plant life grow. As a result, maps are now listing several contiguous areas in and around what they call "Montrose Point." The Magic Hedge is a smaller birding site that is part of this larger area.

The flora consists of a group of unrelated bushes and trees on a point in the park that extends a short distance out into the lake. It is also known as the "Chicago Point Pelee," so called for its similarity to the thin, long peninsula in Ontario, Canada, that extends down into Lake Erie. In the Hedge, a fascinating variety of species of migrating birds perch, jabber and find sustenance on their migration north or south. Here also are other birders, who often are more than willing to offer suggestions and sighting information. In fact, the most notable feature of the Hedge is the number of people standing around with binoculars.

Watch for: Warblers (including worm-eating, hooded), snow bunting, rock wren, Pacific loon and groove-billed ani.

3. The Indiana Dunes Lakeshore National Park

This 10-mile length of seashore and dunes along Lake Michigan's Indiana shoreline is broken up in stretches by industrial and residential structures. In the places where the land is public, and even sometimes where it is still industrial, there exists one of the major birds havens in North America.

The unusual habitats of the dunes share characteristics with such varied ecological landscapes as beach, desert, tundra, grasslands, woods, bog, farm, swamp and prairie. Species can be spotted here that range from the tiny titmouse to the two-foot–tall great horned owl. One of many little joys for the birder is approaching a killdeer's nest, listening to its distress cry and watching the bird's "broken wing" act, which it performs to ward off intruders.

Watch for: Carolina wrens along Beverly Drive, jaegers along the lakefront, warblers (blue-winged, prairie, Kentucky, hooded) and great blue herons in secluded marsh areas near the lake.

The O'Hare
mud flats

4. The Mud Flats

Located just south of O'Hare International Airport, the mud flats are near the entrance to the large postal facility on Irving Park Road west of Mannheim Road. Don't bother to go if there has been a heavy rain, for the area will have turned into a lake, with a few ducks being the only visitors. But under the right conditions, the birder can enjoy watching shorebirds as in few other places in the area. The scenery includes planes taking off and landing at O'Hare.

Watch for: As many as 12 species of shorebirds.

5. The Lake Calumet Region

This too-long-ignored body of water in an industrial area along I-90 on the far South Side of the city is a special place for a number of egrets, herons and other rare shorebirds. During one "bird-a-thon," a single individual spotted 111 species of birds in a single day.

Among those which have been seen here are Wilson's phalarope, greater and lesser yellow legs, semi-palmated plover, little blue herons and snowy egrets. Much of the area has yet to be upgraded to its potential, but it contains what *Tribune* reporter Jon Anderson labeled "pockets of wonder." Birding stops might include Burnham Prairie, the Big Marsh, the Hegewisch Marsh, Dead Stick Pond and Indian Ridge Marsh as well as Lake Calumet itself. Along the edges of Lake Calumet is one of the largest gull-nesting colonies in the Midwest.

Great white egret and hatchlings at the Lake Renwick Heron Rookery (Will County Forest Preserves)

Watch for: Rarer gulls (glaucous, Iceland), godwits (marbled, Hudsonian) and greater yellowlegs.

6. Illinois Beach State Park

This 829-acre preserve lies between Lake Michigan and the Union Pacific Railroad tracks in Zion. The area south of the park facilities offers dunes, cattail marshes, sand ridges and swales. The walk south from the lodge follows a birding trail that overlooks the Dead River.

This river-marsh area is an environment with a short, go-nowhere body of water and a wide variety of migrating and nesting species. These include meadowlarks, snow geese, black terns, ospreys and eastern screech owls. A bird list is available at the nature center near the beginning of the trail. The park also has another section to the north, separated from the lodge area by the Zion Nuclear Energy Plant. This area provides its birds with various habitats that include marshes, wetlands, prairies, ponds, a lakefront and, of course, dunes.

During the fall this park is one of the best locations in the entire area to observe hawk migration, either from the observation towers just north

THE BIRDS OF CHICAGOLAND: TEN PLACES TO ENJOY THEM

of where the Dead River meets the lake or at the North Unit near Camp Logan.

Watch for: Whistling swans and some rarer gulls (glaucous, laughing, great black-backed, Iceland).

7. Lake Renwick Heron Rookery Nature Preserve

An island in this Will County nature preserve in Plainfield is the nesting site for five species of birds. These are the double-crested cormorants, small cattle egrets, great blue herons, great egrets and the state-endangered-listed black-crowned night-herons. The island and its trees are full of these birds in motion—learning to fly, taking off, landing, wading and diving for fish.

As recently as 1990 this was not a sanctuary, but rather a privately owned gravel quarry. Now, in order to protect the nesting pairs, times for observing them are highly restricted. The rookery is open to visitors from May through August and only for one hour early on Wednesday mornings and for four hours on Saturday mornings.

A person can view the rookery at all times from a distance by pulling off Route 30 (Plainfield Road) at any of several locations across from the rookery.

Watch for: Breeding egrets, herons and cormorants.

8. The Skokie Lagoons

Once called the Skokie Marsh, these lie along the east side of the Edens I-94 Expressway in an area that extends from Dundee Road south to Willow Road. In the 1930s, the WPA's Civil Conservation Corps turned the area into a series of small, interconnected lakes, properly referred to as lagoons. They offer an opportunity for people to hike and see marshes, woods and wetland habitats. The many species they attract include egrets and herons. The preserve also offers a canoe launch, allowing people to paddle through this nature area, where humans are often more scarce than other animals. The waterways are alive with geese, ducks and shorebirds, while the woods are full of the flight paths and songs of a variety of migrating and nesting birds. The lagoon-woods environment permits visitors to be in a forest setting without its leaves and

SOME ADDITIONAL CHICAGO WILDERNESS BIRDING AREAS

a. Waukegan Harbor

b. Crabtree Farm Nature Center—Three miles southwest of Barrington

c. Morton Arboretum—Lisle

d. Lincoln Park—Chicago

e. Gilson Park—Wilmette

f. Northwestern University landfill

g. Navy Pier—Chicago

h. Grant Park and the Lakefront, especially around the Museum Campus—Chicago

i. Eggers Woods—West of the Illinois-Indiana line on 112th Street

j. Wolf Lake—South Side, Chicago. South on Avenue "O"

k. Powder Horn Swamp—South of Hegewisch at 134th Street

l. Sand Ridge Nature Center—South of South Holland, U.S. 6 at Paxton Avenue

m. Pilcher Park & Bird Haven—East Side of Joliet, just off U.S. 30

n. The Illinois and Michigan Canal Towpath

o. Goose Lake Prairie State Park—Southwest of Joliet

branches crackling beneath their feet and scaring off the forest birds. The Chicago Botanic Garden, just to the north, provides not only ample bodies of water for visiting birds but also bushes and trees with berries and nuts to attract them.

Watch for: Mergansers, loons, least bitterns, terns and owls.

9. The Wooded Island or Paul Douglas Nature Preserve

This island is located south of the Museum of Science and Industry in Jackson Park. It was designed by Frederick Law Olmsted and served as part of the 1893 World's Columbian Exposition. The island has been one of the most popular bird observation sites in Chicago for more than a century. The preserve is named for the late U.S. Senator Paul H. Douglas, a long-time Hyde Park resident. His interest in nature was key to the Indiana Dunes becoming a national shoreline park.

The birds like the food afforded by the woods, the many plants of the Osaka Garden on the island, the surrounding lagoons and nearby Lake Michigan. Audubon board member Doug Anderson has led morning bird walks on the island during the peak migrations in April, May, September and October.

Watch for: Screech owl, harlequin duck, bufflehead, Townsend's warbler and bohemian waxwing.

10. The Area's Rivers

These include the Chicago, the Calumet, the Illinois, the Skokie, the Des Plaines and the Fox. Also noteworthy are Salt Creek, the Cal-Sag Channel, the North Shore Channel, and the Chicago Sanitary and Ship Canal. Each serves as a pathway for birds traveling through the area to and from the Mississippi flyway.

The best spots of the rivers are often near dams such as the Des Plaines River Dam Number 1 (northeast of the Palwaukee Airport) and Number 2 (east of Milwaukee Road and north of Willow Road). At a dam on the North Branch of the Chicago River (just north of Argyle Street) two birders reported seeing nine black-crowned night-herons at one time. Even when the birding is not as rewarding as it usually is, the scenery still presents delightful surprises at almost every bend in the river, canal, creek or channel.

During the fall migration, warblers, swallows and nighthawks can be seen in large numbers catching insects along the canal.

Watch for: The pileated woodpecker along the Des Plaines River; the vermilion flycatcher, cinnamon teal, and the yellow-throated and black-throated gray warblers along the North Shore Channel

▌12. The Tallgrass Prairies of the
CHICAGO AREA:
WORKS IN PROGRESS

The prairie is not so much a place as it is an experience. It's an ever-changing kaleidoscope of brilliantly colored flowers and plumed grasses waving in the wind.

—ILLINOIS DEPARTMENT OF TRANSPORTATION POSTER

In the tallgrass prairies, especially in late summer and early fall, Nature seems to be in her most effervescent mood. She seems to cry out exuberantly, inviting all to behold her glorious garments.

Thanks to eco-pioneers, volunteers and government agencies, this charming display has begun to return to many places throughout northern Illinois, where Dame Nature's voice once rang out loud and clear.

Featuring plants with such intriguing names as rattlesnake master, compass plant, shooting star, gay feather and big bluestem, the bright-flowered prairies have recreated a beauty that once was anything but rare in this area.

Prairie was the name the French used for the meadows outside of Paris. The early explorers were at a loss to find any other term to describe the tall, waving expanses of flowers and grass they beheld in the Midwest.

Technically, they are grasslands. It is the great height of the specific grasses in them that give them their character and name. In the spring, when the

Prarie gayfeather shoot upward among rosin weed and other enthusiastic prarie plants (Torkel Korling estate)

grasses are still shoots, it is difficult to distinguish among them. As the season continues and their heads take form, it becomes easier. The most prevalent Illinois prairie grass is the big bluestem, whose head in late fall resembles a turkey foot.

Prairie root systems can be eight feet deep and represent one of the oldest living things on earth. Their grasses and flowering plants support an ecosystem quite unlike that of any other habitat, with abundant species of insects, birds and small mammals.

Native Americans, who once lived among the tallgrass prairie plants, developed healing and medicinal uses for many of them. Early pioneers, and later nineteenth and twentieth century herbalists, rediscovered such uses for a number of plants and roots.

In recent decades, individuals began to recognize prairie patches and considered them interesting and quite lovely. They found them on untilled parts of farms, along railroad tracks and in other out-of-the-way places.

Within the last ten to 15 years, this appreciation has intensified. The number of volunteers working with prairies has increased geometrically. The list of individuals professionally qualified to develop a prairie has also grown dramatically. Townspeople, neighbors, and high school students—an army of volunteers—have helped restore or plant prairies throughout Chicago, its suburbs, parks, forest preserves, rural areas and back yards.

"THE UNPRAIRIE STATE"

Illinois' official nickname is "The Prairie State." Some ecologists, however, have started calling it "The Unprairie State," because it has lost more than 99% of the habitat which once carpeted it with tall grasses and wildly beautiful flowers.

These efforts have meant considerable grunt work, which includes picking weeds, identifying plants and gathering seeds, as well as the annual burning necessary to get rid of Eurasian non-prairie plants.

A deep understanding of nature in the Midwest must begin with an understanding of the tallgrass prairies, which carpeted much of the area two hundred years ago.

In the days when Native Americans dwelt along the area rivers, local habitats also included wetlands, wooded riverbanks, forests and oak savannas. Still, the prairies stretched farther than the eye could see and covered much of the Chicago Lakeplain as well as much of the rest of the northern part of the state.

These fields, teeming with interdependent life forms, represented the ecosystem of this area for thousands of years—since the receding of the glaciers.

The prairies helped shape the spirituality and daily lives of the Native Americans. Nature gave them an environment that was healthy, full of wild flowers and oxygen-creating plants. These, they treated as companions and friends with whom they shared a special bond. They belonged not only to the land, but also to the plants, birds, insects, and small animals that also lived off of it. They understood that there was a relationship of life connecting them to it.

For such reasons, the tallgrass prairie has been called sacred.

Black-eyed Susans proliferate in a patch of prarie (Torkel Korling estate)

Yet the prairie seemed to be a nemesis to the pioneers wanting to grow corn and wheat. The tallgrass prairie ecosystem had greatly enriched Midwestern soil, which is why people hurried here in wagons and by ship from New England, where the rocks had been many and the land wanting. But to get at the rich soil, the new arrivals had to cut through the prairie's tough grassy covering or *sward*.

These farmers were blind to the reality that the tallgrass ecosystem bespoke a cycle of life forever turning. Neither storm nor flood nor fire had

THE BEAUTY OF THE CHICAGO WILDERNESS

MEASURING THE LOSS

The tallgrass prairies have been more than decimated. While some 75% of the world's rainforests have been destroyed, a whopping 99.3% chunk of the Illinois tallgrass prairies is gone.

A display at the new Peggy Notebaert Nature Museum calls attention to the fact that only 0.07% of the prairie remains. To demonstrate how significant this is, it makes the comparison with money: if a person had $100, 0.07% of it would be 7 cents. It's an apt reference, because the $100 is a symbol for abundance. The 7 cents represents the poverty of today's ecosystem, once a colorful sea of tall grasses and flowers.

Scientists have little idea what losing so much of the Midwest's ecosystem will mean to the soil, the oxygen supply, the waterways, animal life, birds and human life in 100 or 500 years.

---

been able to choke off its ancient, abundant life forms. The steel plow, however, succeeded.

Writing in the Spring 1999 issue of *Chicago Wilderness,* Alex Blumberg said it well:

> For 10,000 years, the Midwestern prairie soil, like a thrifty pensioner, set aside more carbon than it spent. Then along came the steel moldboard plow and blew the savings virtually overnight.

As a result of the pioneers turned farmers, not a prairie in Illinois today is large enough that it can sustain a single pair of prairie-dependent birds.

Botanists have yet to learn the impact on the environment made by the botanic cataclysm that has destroyed the tallgrass prairie. This is one of the strong reasons for preserving an ecosystem such as the tallgrass prairies, oak savannas and wetlands.

Individual prairie plants are hosts for species-specific animals, insects and birds. To understand the forms of life dependent on the grasses and flowers that grow there, one need but step into a prairie, listen and observe.

A specific example is the regal fritillary butterfly. It has long been listed as threatened simply because its food sources, such as the leadplant and bird's foot violet that are found in tallgrass prairies, have become rare. Baltimore checkerspots and swamp metalmarks similarly rely on what are now uncommon wetland plants.

The prairie's crusty, tough and tangled roots have effectively protected the fertile earth from erosion and windstorms, such those that hit the dust bowl areas of the United States in the 1930s. The prairie roots are no longer around to conserve the soil of the Midwest.

Fortunately, the prairies appear to be on their way back, albeit quite tenuously.

They are at this point but tiny, almost unnoticeable areas of beauty. Still, they remain decidedly alive, carrying a message from the past and a hope for the future.

Here are ten of the special areas where people have been working to bring back tallgrass prairies.

1. Goose Lake Prairie State Park.

> *Near Morris, Ill., west of I-55 and south of the Illinois River.*

THEIR FORMER GLORY

The tallgrasses of the Midwest prairies were described by the early settlers as growing higher than a man on horseback and flaming as bright with color as a spinning sun.

Goose Lake Prairie State Park is beautiful, but not everyone seems to find it so.

The park, which has 2,537 acres of large tallgrass prairie, is the most extensive fully restored prairie in Illinois and one of the largest in the county.

The nearby Midewin prairie is far larger, but it will take a generation or more for it to be restored completely.

Isabel S. Abrams, in her book *The Nature of Chicago* (Chicago Review Press, 1997), describes Goose Lake in almost lyrical terms:

> Take the tallgrass nature trail to see eight-to-twelve-foot-high cordgrass, big bluestem, Indian grass, and forbs that bloom and paint the prairie with changing colors through the season.

In their *Chicagoland & Beyond: Nature and History Within 200 Miles* (Hippocrene Books, 1992), Gerald and Patricia Gutek are more prosaic in their description. They write:

> Although Goose Lake Prairie may be described as interesting instead of beautiful, it has many rewards for the naturalist.

The book adds:

> Goose Lake is an interesting site for naturalists, but its charms are subtle and would not particularly appeal to younger children.

The great nineteenth century landscape designer Frederick Law Olmsted, on the other hand, obviously celebrated such subtlety. He writes of the kind of beauty one finds, for example, in the tallgrass prairie:

> Dame Nature is a gentle woman. No guide's fees will obtain her favor, nor abrupt demand; hardly will she bear questioning, or direct gazing at her beauty; least of all will she reveal it truly to

Entrance to the Midewin National Tallgrass Prairie (Forest Service photo)

the hurried glance of a passing traveler . . . always we must quietly and patiently wait upon her. Gradually and silently the charm comes over us, the beauty has entered our souls. We know not exactly when nor how, but going away we remember it with a tender, subdued, filial like joy.

Goose Lake Prairie State Park offers seven miles of trails. It also has a glacial pond, a picnic area, a log cabin dating to 1834, guided tours and several elevated points from which to view the sweeping panorama.

2. The Midewin National Tallgrass Prairie

> *Straight south of Joliet off U.S. Hwy 53; look for the marker pictured above on the east side of the road.*

The Midewin Prairie, at an estimated 19,000 acres, is enormous. It is the site of what was formerly the Joliet Arsenal, an industrial complex that for decades manufactured munitions.

On Feb. 10, 1996, President Clinton signed the Illinois Land Conservation Act, which mandated that the area be turned into a national tallgrass prairie park, a national veterans cemetery, a county landfill and two industrial parks. The USDA Forest Service was named to manage the prairie; the Department of Veteran Affairs, the cemetery; and Will County, the landfill.

"Midewin" (pronounced *mi-DAY-win*) is the word the Potawatomis used for their "healing society," which was made up of individuals who used rituals, sacred objects and prairie plants to treat sick people. The Field Museum of Natural History has a superb first floor display of the items, ceremonies and procedures the Midewin healing society used throughout this region.

This name was chosen for the site to express the hope that that the prairie could help the area to heal itself, making up for the use and abuse it received as an arsenal and weapon-making complex.

It will take a long time for Midewin to reach its potential as a fully-restored prairie. One spokesman suggested the year 2020, but the transformation will likely take a decade or two longer than that.

Most areas are large empty fields, many of which were used for farming or grazing. Other areas, protected by high fences, served as buffer zones for the now-defunct munitions factories.

The process has begun in earnest to restore these lands to their original prairie status. It is not enough to plant the seeds of prairie plants. Other vital procedures, described as "plowed ground restoration," will take years. It is necessary to restore not only the plants, but also the soil itself and the microscopic organisms in it that were rooted out by plowing.

What makes Midewin so important is that it will be so vast that visitors and various animals can experience the prairies the way their ancestors did—as a rich and seemingly endless expanse of natural beauty.

In March 2000, the USDA Forest Service honored the volunteers of Midewin with three separate national awards. Those chosen for recognition included: Portia Blume-Gallegos, the prairie's volunteer coordinator; 60 associates from Toyota Motor USA Inc.'s regional sales office, who helped gather native plant seeds and build fences; and students from nine Will County schools.

Altogether, more than 600 individuals had volunteered a total of 8,300 hours to the Midewin program, contributing their time and talents to such projects as monitoring plants, streams and wildlife; leading environmental workshops; and caring for the native seed gardens.

Because of the U.S. Army's ongoing cleanup of contaminated areas, public access to Midewin continues to be restricted. Guided tours of some areas are available. These focus on wildflowers, birding, geology and the history of the prairie.

The phone number for arranging such interpretative visits is 815-523-6370. The web site for additional information is www.fs.fed.us/mntp.

3. The Suzanne S. Dixon Prairie

The Chicago Botanic Garden: on Lake-Cook Road, east of the Edens I-94 Expressway.

The Dixon Prairie, located on the far south end of the Botanic Garden, includes 250 plant species. It is unique in the United States because it consists of six reconstructed prairie communities. They are:

- *Mesic Prairie:* This is a typical tallgrass prairie, with rich black soil often dominated by the most common of the grasses, big bluestem. Other species include rattlesnake master, prairie dock and northern dropseed.

- *Bur Oak Savanna:* Plants that grow in the shade of the trees include shooting star, plain Indian plantain and purple Joe Pye weed.

- *Wet Prairie:* This is a marsh area usually inundated with water in spring and summer. Typical species are cord grass, Riddell's goldenrod, blue joint grass and ironweed.

- *Fen:* These are wetlands characterized by oozing water. Its unusual chemistry comes from its soil, which is peat with a high concentration of lime. Its plants, tolerant of these conditions, include various sedges, fringed gentian, grass of parnassus and bog goldenrod.

- *Gravel Hill Prairie:* This area has slopes of dry, sandy and gravely soil. This prairie has little bluestem rather than big, scuffy pea and dwarf blazing star.

- *Sand Prairie:* This is a low dune prairie of the kind found along Lake Michigan. It is sand in the forms of swells (dunes) and swales (the area in between). Among the species it supports are lake shore rush, Ohio goldenrod, Kalm's St. John's wort, little bluestem and sky blue aster.

Suzanne S. Dixon Prairie (Chicago Botanic Garden/Linda Oyama Bryan)

4. The Santa Fe Prairie

A 10.8-acre site in southwestern Cook County. It is in an industrial park bordered by I-55 along the north and I-294 on the south. Its immediate borders are Des Plaines River frontage road and the Burlington Northern/Santa Fe railroad tracks.

This pristine prairie site was discovered in 1946 by plant taxonomist Floyd Swink, author of *Plants of the Chicago Region* (The Morton Arboretum, 1969). This work, on the shelf of every Chicago-area plant biologist, names more than 2,000 species of vascular plants, both native and introduced, that can be found growing wild in this region.

This find was unusually important for Swink and all who appreciate tall-grass prairies. It was one of only three grade-A mesic and dry gravel prairies listed in the 1979 Illinois Natural Area Inventory. One of the others, according to Alex Blumberg in *Chicago Wilderness,* has since been destroyed. Santa Fe is the larger "of the two remaining in Illinois, perhaps in the world."

In the mid-1960s, biologist Dr. Robert Betz convinced the Santa Fe Railroad not to develop the land. Thirty years later, volunteers from the Illinois & Michigan Canal National Historic Corridor Civic Center Authority helped block access to the site by off-road vehicles, which had been racing there and doing damage to the site. They also began restoring the degraded area.

5. The Ashburn Prairie

Marquette Park at 67th Street and Kedzie Avenue.

A movie ought to be made about this one.

The storyline would be great. Led by the Chicago Park District, students and other local volunteers helped move a half acre of prairie and its massive root system to a new location.

This seemingly impossible task was accomplished with machines used to dig out and move trees. Because of the great depth to which prairie grass roots grow, these tree spades needed to cut blocks of soil eight feet deep and six feet in diameter. They then had to be lifted on trucks and shipped to the new location.

THE BEAUTY OF THE CHICAGO WILDERNESS

The volunteers had to separate out the flowers and prepare them for the journey. It was a labor-intensive, dirty and delicate job. It succeeded, however, and one of the city's last surviving prairies was saved.

6. Gensburg-Markham Prairie Preserve

Off Whipple Avenue, two blocks north of 159th Street in Markham.

Because Gensburg-Markham contains a range of ecosystems from mesic to sand prairie and sedge meadow, it offers an unusual array of plants and birds.

It is partially a virgin prairie, one that has been expanded beyond its core. This field of native grasses and flowers was found in the 1960s by Northeastern Illinois University molecular biologist Dr. Robert Betz, while on a walk after dinner.

The Gensburg family of Markham owned the land on which Betz discovered the prairie. In 1971, they donated 60 acres of their land to the Nature Conservancy.

Today, it is a National Natural Landmark.

If you want to hear one of the worst-singing birds in the world, listen for the rare Henslow's sparrow, which nests here. It has been called "the poorest vocalist of any bird," one which has "an undistinguished hiccoughing SLICK."

This bird has recently been moved from the "threatened" to the more serious "endangered list." The reason is that it takes 125 acres of open grassland to support a healthy population of Henslow's sparrows.

7. The Schulenberg Prairie.

Morton Arboretum: on Hwy 53 just north of I-88 and the East-West Tollway

The Morton Arboretum's 55 acres of prairie are fittingly named after Ray Schulenberg, who maintained and developed them from their establishment in 1962. He is now retired, but his interest, concern and experimentation made this area "the region's archetypical proving ground for the

Schulenberg Prairie (Morton Arboretum)

kind of restoration that starts with nothing but the soil," according to Ray Wiggers in *Chicago Wilderness* (Summer 2000).

Some prairies in the area were discovered and nurtured to health. These include the Santa Fe Prairie, Gensburg-Markham Prairie and the H.U.M. Prairie (along with a railroad-based Kane County trail that goes through the towns of Huntley, Union and Merengo). Others, such as the Suzanne S. Dixon Prairie at the Chicago Botanic Garden, were not. The Schulenberg site had long served as farmland. What its caretaker learned through trial and error was eventually passed along to almost everyone in the Midwest who has now worked in prairie restoration.

Schulenberg still sees the prairie as a work in progress after 38 years. "There are still many prairie plant species lacking from it," he has noted.

Today, the Schulenberg Prairie is special for another reason. It has an oak savanna adjacent to it, recalling the mixture of similar but diverse ecosystems of the area's past.

8. The Fermilab Prairie

Batavia: north off I-88 on Farnsworth/Kirk Road to the entrance on Pine Street.

The Fermilab prairie restoration project is a good experience waiting to happen. It is large, beautiful, and still developing.

Fermilab's 1,100 acres can define a prairie in a way that little ones, even vibrant, virgin ones, cannot.

The man whose name repeatedly comes up in the stories of Midwest prairie restoration is Dr. Robert Betz. He was a key figure in this project, but so were many others. Fermilab staff and hundreds of volunteers have helped by hand-collecting seeds in the fall so they could be used as the prairie developed further.

This process, which nature herself once took care of, has become more and more complex in recent years. The lessons learned by trial and error at the Morton Arboretum are being employed and refined as this much larger acreage at Fermilab is restored. The enemy is Eurasian plants that grow in abundance once the earth is turned by a plow. The soil has to be reconditioned to favor prairie plants over such weeds. At the Fermilab they are doing just that and creating one of the largest, most beautiful prairie canvases in the Midwest.

9. James Woodworth Prairie Preserve (Peacock Prairie)

Niles: on the east side of Milwaukee Avenue, two blocks north of Greenleaf.

Prairies have their stories, their history. This small, five-acre site was once part of the Peacock farm. In the 1960s, the site became a miniature golf course and a go cart track. It was first named the Peacock Prairie, but is now called the James Woodworth Prairie Preserve after the tenth mayor of Chicago, an ancestor of the man who contributed the money to build an interpretative center there.

A section of the Peacock farm was wetter in the spring than the cultivated area around it. At that spot, according to descendants of the people who farmed this land, no plow had ever cracked the sward of the prairie because it was harder to get at.

In the 1960s, a group of individuals banded together under the name of the Peacock Prairie Preservation Committee and worked with the Openlands Project. The acres were deeded in 1968 to the University of Illinois, Chicago, which now owns and manages it.

At first the university administrators simply fenced it off and would not allow the burning necessary for prairie development. Eventually, they changed their minds. Since then, the school has opened an interpretative center and the prairie now has both brochures and signs available to help visitors.

10. Shaw Woodlands and Prairie

Off Green Bay Road in Lake Forest. Turn west on Laurel Avenue (two long blocks north of Deerpath Road); parking is at the end of the street.

This triangular piece of land is tucked away in Lake Forest, bordered by the Deerpath Country Club to the south, the Union Pacific Railroad to the west and the Skokie River to the east. It features one of the most charming tallgrass prairies in the Chicago area. It also includes, adjacent to the prairie: Shaw Woods, Stevenson Savanna, A. B. Dick River Trail and Bennett Meadow. The area is maintained by the Lake Forest Open Lands Association.

The combination of trails, savanna, meadow, river, bordering woods, railroad and individual grasses make it the kind of prairie that will delight any visitor.

One irony is that, unlike the virgin prairies of pioneer days, an occasional golf ball can be found along its edges.

It is a beautiful prairie in the late summer and fall, when its flowers are in bloom and its grasses are their full height. Its charm is also there in winter and early spring, when its color is brown and its promise is the greatest.

13. Hiking and Cycling in the
CHICAGO AREA:
THROUGH DUNE,
PRAIRIE AND FOREST

In wilderness is the preservation of the world.

—HENRY DAVID THOREAU

If they could do so conveniently, many people would travel outside the Chicago area to experience the wonders of nature. They would go to the mountains or the seashore, where nature, they believe, is far more dramatic and majestic.

Gradually, however, people can grow to appreciate the subtler beauty of the Chicago Wilderness. Time and experience help them to discover that in this region there are special places, areas where, as Tony Hiss writes in *Prairie Passage* (University of Illinois Press, 1998), "awe lingers."

For some, this process of discovery occurs without much work on their part. They walk out of their doors and are already close to a forest, prairie or dune. But for most, some effort is required. They must seek nature out.

The bicycling and hiking trails of the Chicago area afford them the opportunity to do just that.

Nearly 200 years ago, a young apprentice fur trader named Gurdon Saltonstall Hubbard discovered that hiking could expand his appreciation of the

THE HABITATS OF THE NATIONAL LAKESHORE

This relatively small area contains a stunning list of habitats: sand dune, swell and swale, desert (complete with prickly pear cactus), bog, dry and wet prairie, river flood plain and mesophytic forests.

area's quiet natural beauty. He arrived at Chicago in 1818, long before it was even a village. The Native Americans called him *Papamatabe* or "Swift Walker" after he hiked an unbelievable distance to deliver medicine and food to a Native American village that had been cut off by frigid weather.

In his autobiography, Hubbard wrote with spiritual overtones of life in an area of rivers, marshes, tallgrass prairies and woodlands. His transcendent effort is reminiscent of W. H. Hudson's *Green Mansions*, the classic novel set in the rainforests of Brazil.

Now, in the twenty-first century, modern-day Gurdon Hubbards have started to rediscover the Chicago Wilderness as a lovely, loveable place that can directly touch the soul.

Here are ten of the trails or hiking areas that take one to many of the special places in the Chicago Wilderness:

1. The Indiana Dunes National Lakeshore

One to two hours east of Chicago.

In their book *Wild Lake Michigan* (Voyageur Press, Inc., 1997), John and Ann Mahan write:

> To walk in the dunes is to walk through time. These miniscule grains of quartz that gather together to make such a magnificent community were created long before the coming of humans. Children of the glacier and wards of the wind, they have for millennia washed and drifted, bounced and tumbled from one age to the next.

J. Ronald Engel writes:

> For countless years the waves have thundered upon the beach and the ripples have murmured along it. The music is recorded in the sand.

The Indiana Dunes National Lakeshore was the first urban area to join Yosemite, the Rocky Mountains, the Everglades and the Grand Canyon as a national park. Like them it has proved a place of unexpected delight and deep personal discovery.

At first, the dunes do not seem especially impressive. They consist of a beach on the southern rim of Lake Michigan, and sandy hills extending up to ten miles inland. The hills support intermittent patches of vegetation barely holding on to life.

This national park, furthermore, is in a less-than-enchanting area of Northern Indiana. It is bordered on the west and south by factories, steel mills and scraggly orchards.

Yet, to those who look closer, a gentle, inner beauty presents itself. The dunes are rich with rare natural habitats that can surprise and stun a visitor.

Jean Komaiko and Norma Shaeffer express the magic of the area in their 1973 book *Doing the Dunes:*

> In scale the National Lakeshore is small so that, in effect, it represents a sheltered refuge. It requires the visitor to forsake modern transportation and go afoot to experience its delights. By tramping its dunes, walking its beaches, feeling its north wind, blowing sand, moist heat and biting cold, smelling its faint marsh sour and the perfume of its fields, and quietly examining its vast profusion of flowers, trees, insects and birds, the visitor can begin to construct the world that existed before man intruded.

The dunes are the result of consistent northwesterly winds blowing over the lake for the last 10,000 years. These winds have carried the sand and dropped it in front of older inland dunes and hills. As this process continued, more and more hills and ridges were created. Now, the older, stable dunes are as far as 10 miles inland, while the ones closer to the lake are still in formation.

A MONUMENTAL DISCOVERY

To appreciate the full significance of the dunes and their place in nature, it helps to revisit an incident that occurred a little over 100 years ago. Botanist Dr. Henry Chandler Cowles was passing by on a train to Chicago and saw the dunes through his window. He was so startled to see an unusual but ordered mixture of plant species growing together that he got off at the next stop and went back to study them. It was then that he realized each dune had its own unique selection of plants.

This discovery has been compared to Darwin's visit to the Galapagos Islands, which triggered his formulation of the theory of natural selection in the animal kingdom. Over the next five years (1896–1901), Dr. Cowles became the first to understand and expound the idea of *plant succession.*

These theories explain that a single area will be home to a series of different plant communities, which will succeed one another in an orderly and progressive sequence. For example, in order for flowers and trees to grow in a seemingly barren area, certain grasses and other simple vegetation must first struggle for survival there and enrich the soil.

Dr. Cowles joined the faculty of the University of Chicago, and thus was able to spend the rest of his years studying plant life in the dunes.

THE BEAUTY OF THE CHICAGO WILDERNESS

DUNES AND THEIR STAGES

Scientists note stages in the development of the dune, ones that can be easily noted on a hike. The first is the *storm beach*, represented by the relatively level, sandy shoreline. The next is the *foredune*, which has no soil, but some plant life. The third is the *pine dune*, which has a thin layer of soil from decaying vegetation. The fourth is the *oak dune*, with a slightly thicker layer of soil. And finally there is the *beech-maple dune*. It enjoys a deep, rich carpet of earth beneath it.

"Going afoot" is indeed the best way to appreciate the ancient beauty of the dunes. Many Indiana dunes areas have notable nature trails:

- The West Beach/Ogden Dunes area is served by the Ogden Dunes station of the South Shore Line railroad (listed in the phone book as the "Northern Indiana Commuter Transportation District"). Its West Beach Trail leads to Long Lake and the Long Lake Wetland. The key path is the strenuous one-mile West Beach Succession Trail. It is possibly the best place in the dunes to witness the plant succession that so inspired Dr. Cowles. The Inland Marsh Trail (south off Highway 12) introduces hikers to the marsh, and to a dune area vastly different from and far older than those nearer the lake.

- Another series of inland paths leads off from the Bailly/Chelberg Information Center on Highway 20 and Mineral Springs Road. These trails afford opportunities to encounter the Bailly Homestead log cabin and the nearby Bailly Cemetery, which served the early settlers of the area.

- Leading off from the Visitor Center on Kemil Road between Highways 12 and 20 are two more dune paths, Calumet Trail and Ly-co-ki-we Trail.

- The State Park's ten trails offer opportunities to climb three massive dunes, Mt. Tom, Mt. Holden and Mt. Jackson, as well as a choice of paths that traverse a great variety of natural dune habitats along the shoreline.

- The Mt. Baldy Trail is in a lakeshore area between Beverly Shores and Michigan City. Getting up this sandy hill can be a struggle, but is worth it for the view. The most amazing fact about Mt. Baldy is that it moves up to four feet a year, gradually burying the oak forest behind it. When was the last time the reader ascended a mountain that was moving at such a rate?

2. Illinois Beach State Park

Along the shore of Lake Michigan 60 miles to the north of Chicago.

Here also are sand dunes. The land is flatter, however, and the walking much easier than in Indiana. Just to the southwest of the park lodge is a nature center, where an individual can learn about the unique environments found in the area.

There are two reminders that this area is part desert. The first is some cactus plants. The second is the historical fact that, in the era of silent films, cowboys "rode the range" here—Chicago's early movie industry used these dunes to simulate the Wild West.

The terrain consists of a series of sand ridges interspersed with marshes, which parallel the shoreline of Lake Michigan.

A second, separate area of the park just to north of the City of Zion also affords dunes, marshes, ponds, wetlands, hiking trails and birding. Walking north from this area transports the hiker into an environment full of surprises because it is not the usual forest, river or prairie habitat of the Chicago area. It is not beach, although it once was, but thriving marsh and scraggly bush—a lush world of its own.

3. The Illinois and Michigan Canal Towpath

Part of the Illinois and Michigan Canal Heritage Corridor. The trailhead is at the Chicago Portage National Historic Site on the west side of Harlem Avenue just north of I-55. For the most part, the developed hiking trails stretch over the western 20 miles of the Corridor, with plans for them to be continued eastward to Chicago.

No historic site in the area has received as much attention and development in the last decade as "The Corridor." The Illinois and Michigan Canal followed this historic route from 1848 until well into the twentieth century. The Corridor is also known as the Chicago Outlet Valley, since thousands of years ago it was a gorge/waterway through which a massive amount of water regularly flowed.

Today, these paths still offer some of the wildest, most engaging natural scenery within hundreds of miles of Chicago.

The trees are worth noting. Oak and hickory stand proud on high bluffs. White pine, cedar, Canadian yew, partridgeberry and bunchberry can be seen along the lower trails, as can an occasional beaver or coyote.

An eco-history park in Lockport and a canal museum at Utica across the river from Starved Rock State Park offer interpretative information that helps make a hike or bicycle ride on the path more meaningful. These are just two of the eight official visitor centers along the Corridor.

The trail lends itself especially well to biking, as many of the cities along the route have paths through them clearly marked for cyclers.

Site on the South Fork of the South Branch of the Chicago River where the I & M Canal originated (Commission on Chicago Landmarks)

THE ILLINOIS AND MICHIGAN CANAL

This waterway, man-made in the mid-1800s, established Chicago as "the port on the prairie" and brought prosperity and jobs to an area extending from Lake Michigan to the Illinois River at LaSalle and Peru.

The canal had 15 locks, three dams and four aqueducts. Sections of the towpath still exist. The canal, originally only 15 feet wide, saw men and mules pulling canal boats across its surface. Part of the old canal still has water in it. Most of it does not; much of it is little more than a grown-over trough of vegetation. At Lockport, a few of the locks have been restored.

127

The longest part of the trail extends for 60.5
miles from Channahon in Will County to La
Salle, nearly 100 miles west of the Loop, but
there is also a 2.5-mile section in Lockport and
an 8.9-mile section near Willow Springs in Cook
County.

A visit to one of the interpretative centers or a
book on the path can help the hiker or cyclist
choose an area of the towpath or the Corridor
best suited to individual interests.

4. Palos, Sag Valley and the Little Red School House Nature Center

9800 South Willow Springs Road, Willow Springs.

If they were asked to draw up a list of the great
natural treasures of the Chicago area, many nature lovers would place this vast region near the
top of the list, just after Lake Michigan, the river systems and the dunes.
Yet, to large numbers of Chicago Wilderness residents, the Palos area is little known. They may have visited it once or twice, but seldom do they
fully appreciate its wild beauty and historical significance.

The Palos/Sag Valley Division of the Cook County Forest Preserves consists not only of 12,000 acres of forests, prairies and ponds, but also of
kames, eskers and sloughs, reminders left when the Wisconsin Glacier re-
ceded ten thousand years ago. The forests are filled with some of the most
beautiful wildflowers in the region. The ponds and sloughs afford excellent fishing.

In addition, one finds history here. This area was heavily used by Native
Americans. Their village sites and burial mounds are scattered throughout
the area. Here also pioneers tilled the land, often quite successfully. Their
farm buildings, worn fences, apple tree remnants and gravesites also remain.

At the center of the forest preserve division is the Little Red School House
Nature Center, once a school building for the children of local farmers.
Today, its staff and brochures provide maps and trail advice.

Leading off from the School House Nature Center are several of the most interesting and popular hiking trails of the Palos area.

5. The Illinois Prairie Path

Through DuPage County, from Maywood west to four divergent sites along the Fox River.

HISTORY OF THE ILLINOIS PRAIRIE PATH

The idea for the Illinois Prairie Path came from May Theilgaard Watts, a teacher, naturalist and author. In 1971, it became the first path in Illinois to be designated a National Trail.

The Illinois Prairie Path is 40 miles long and traverses road beds once used by the now-defunct Chicago, Aurora & Elgin Railway, an electric commuter line that served the western suburbs for 56 years.

Without question, hiking or cycling the path is the best way to see DuPage County, because the trail lets its users experience its past, present and future. The trail, especially its southwest Aurora Branch or Batavia Spur, goes through wooded rural areas. The northern stem divides into branches that head toward Geneva and Elgin. They offer walking paths through one of the nation's most rapidly developing urban regions—and one of its most rapidly shrinking nature areas.

This trail is part of a time warp into the region's past that nature lovers need to experience while they still can. Already, it is a greatly different path than it was when it was first developed a little more than 30 years ago.

The first-railroad-to-hiking trail conversion in the region, the path is also the most extensive, interconnected trail system in the Chicago area.

The Prairie Path starts at First Avenue in Maywood and heads west toward the Fox River, splitting into the four forks before arriving there.

6. The Chicago Park District Bikeway

A series of lakefront hiking and cycling paths through the City of Chicago.

Cycling has been a favorite sport and pastime of Chicagoans for a little over a century, but Chicago's cyclists have never had it as good as they do now. The lakefront, for almost the whole length of the city, can now be

POPULAR PATHS

Many residents of North Side neighborhoods or the suburbs "shoot downtown" to take advantage of the cycle paths. A few hardier individuals even walk the entire stretch. Mainly, people get out of their cars or apartments and stroll, run, skate or cycle a part of it. As this route becomes more and more crowded, however, people are beginning to use and appreciate the path south from the Loop.

viewed through the handlebars of a bike—without competition from horses or cars, or the interruption of potholes.

The scenery along these lakefront pathways is ever changing, affording different views of the lake and skyline. Among the unique discoveries along the way are the Theatre on the Lake at Fullerton Avenue, the Chess Pavilion at North Avenue, Navy Pier, Buckingham Fountain, the Museum Campus and the Museum of Science at Industry at 59th Street; and, of course, the many beaches, parks and harbors, as well as the people enjoying them.

The city recently began work to improve the stretch of the Bikeway in Burnham Park south of the Loop, so that individuals from South Shore or Hyde Park can experience the same kind of lakefront trail that North Siders have long enjoyed. The city has also divided the Bikeway into separate cycling and walking paths, making life easier for people in both lanes.

In 2001, the Chicago Transit Authority made changes in rules and upgrades to equipment that allow cyclists to take their bikes on the "L" (except during rush hours), and put them on the front of specially equipped buses on certain routes.

North of the City of Chicago, the cycle path continues, following both park paths and designated city streets. Much of Evanston, including a long stretch of the Northwestern University campus, is ideal for cycling, running or strolling.

The suburbs to the north of Evanston also represent a mixture of park and street routings, although the latter is more prevalent than the former.

7. The North Branch Bicycle Trail

*Along the North Branch of the Chicago River and
the Skokie Lagoons*

Cyclists on this route get a chance to experience something few others ever do: they discover how wild and beautiful nature can be, even within the city limits. For this the riders can thank the river, the canal and more than 50 years of restoration work.

This winding, asphalt cycling path stretches for 20.1 miles. It accommodates hikers, bicyclists and sometimes equestrians. It often provides parallel dirt paths for those on foot or horseback.

The North Branch Trail starts at Peterson and Caldwell Avenues and goes north through the Chicago Botanic Garden in Glencoe.

Multi-color maps of Chicago show the North Branch Trail route as a broad expanse of green. The path passes along or through golf courses, forest preserves and the Skokie Lagoons. The treed areas it traverses include Miami Woods, Linne Woods, Harms Woods and Blue Star Memorial Woods.

The recently refurbished Skokie Lagoons, with their excellent bird- and wildlife, are followed by an even more beautiful ride through the Botanic Garden.

It is a well-used route and the more ambitious bikers can continue their trip north by taking County Line Road east to the Green Bay Trail.

Cyclists can get a Chicagoland Bicycle Map by calling the Chicagoland Bicycle Federation at 312-42-PEDAL.

8. The Green Bay Trail

*Extends for 18 miles from Shorewood Park in Wilmette to the
northern city limits of Lake Bluff.*

Indians, fur trappers and stagecoaches, and later extraordinarily fast electric trains, once traversed that which hiker and cyclist now do.

Few realize that the Green Bay Trail is truly historic. The name of the trail dates to the days of early Chicago when this path united Fort Dearborn in Chicago with Fort Howard in Green Bay, Wisconsin.

The walker or cyclist will at times tread a right-of-way that once served the fastest railroad in the country, the Chicago and North Shore. This electric interurban was the swiftest of interurban trains; it traveled at speeds exceeding 100 miles an hour.

At Highwood, visitors will also pass a modern-day military base, Fort Sheridan, in the process of being dismantled.

This trail, well kept and often asphalt covered, parallels the Metra's North Line tracks and requires those who utilize it to walk through several sometimes-busy trains stations.

If one enjoys looking at large, fashionable estates, no other area path can compare to the Green Bay. It takes those on foot or bike through such affluent areas as Wilmette, Kenilworth, Winnetka, Glencoe, Ravinia, Highland Park, Highwood, Lake Forest and Lake Bluff.

The trail has more appeal than just residential architecture. There are parks, woods, prairies, pathways to the lake, quaint train stations, migratory birds, deer and several elegant North Shore city centers. Among the latter is Lake Forest with its Market Square district, erected in 1916 as the world's first shopping center.

Where the Green Bay Trail ends in Lake Bluff, the North Shore Trail picks up.

9. The Fox River Trail

From Crystal Lake south to Oswego.

Rivers and nature/bicycle paths work well together and the Fox River Trail is excellent proof. The Fox runs north and south, 12 to 25 miles west of the shores of Lake Michigan. As it passes from McHenry through Kane into Kendall County, it displays a natural beauty deeply reminiscent of the area hundreds of years before the arrival of settlers.

Because a wooded river can attract interesting insects such as water skimmers and birds such as the yellow-rumped warbler and the American redstart, this trail is truly a nature path.

It also goes through quaint old river towns such as Elgin, St. Charles, Geneva, Batavia and Aurora.

More significantly, it winds its way through woods and forest preserves including Fox River Shores, Voyager Landing, Tyler Creek, Blackhawk, Tekakwitha and Fabyan.

It meets up with all four western spurs of the Illinois Prairie Path as well as other trails.

The hiker or cyclist will encounter an oak-hickory forest, nature parks, a full-sized windmill, historical and nature markers and, in Elgin and Aurora, riverboat gambling.

Hiking & Biking in the Fox River Valley by Jim Hochesang (Roots & Wings, 1997) is a delightful guide to have in hand when experiencing what it calls "a well-designed and well-maintained 41-mile asphalt trail system."

10. Other Trails

The Chicago Wilderness area has undergone a hard-to-imagine expansion of hiking and cycling trails that has been documented best in the various volumes of Roots & Wings Publications' hiking and biking guides. These guides cover Cook County, Lake County, DuPage County, the Fox River Valley, and McHenry and Kane Counties.

Perusing these, the reader discovers an almost endless number of interesting tidbits, such as:

- *The Grand Illinois Trail* will eventually be a trail system of more than 475 miles through 17 counties to the Mississippi River and back.
- *The Tinley Creek Bicycle Trail* is described in the following notes. Northern section: "One of my favorites. Hilly trail through woodlands and meadow." Southern section: "Loop trail is a good place for beginning bicyclists. Flat terrain with no street crossings."
- Sign noted in the *Merengo Ridge Conservation Area* with a quote from Aldo Leopold's *A Sand County Almanac* (1949):

  We abuse the land because we regard it as a commodity belonging to us. When we see land as a community to which we belong, we may begin to use it with love and respect. There is no other way for man to survive the impact of mechanized man.

14. Chicago's Parks:
Ways in Which They're Coming Back Strong

One feels these visiting reporters always carry their encrusted opinions with them, like patients with hardened arteries. They have never probed Chicago's interior, never walked the grasses of Chicago's parks.

—Albert Halper, *This Is Chicago*

For generations, the Park District provided Chicagoans with something special. Day in and day out, it offered opportunities for beauty and leisure to enrich their lives. The lakefront and neighborhood parks were the flowering oases in a city driven by financial struggle and success.

Chicago's streets were not paved with gold, but its boulevards and parks were lined with greenery and lush with trees and flowers.

Immigrants and other newcomers to Chicago worked hard to survive, but they and their families could put that struggle aside for a little while, and go over to the city park to become people of leisure and appreciators of beauty.

Then, for a period that spanned the last two generations, the city's residents watched their parks become stagnant. The parks went into such a decline that Chicagoans began to fear rather than to love them. The park system had become crippled by a lack of vision and a racism that saw the North Side parks prosper and blossom while inner city and South Side parks were left behind. Gangs seem to own the turf in many neighborhood parks.

Washington Park, Conservatory and Flower Beds, Chicago.
Oldest South Side Park; Area 371 Acres.

Pre–World War I postcard view of Washington Park Conservatory and flower beds

Wide scale political patronage caused lethargy. Chicago Park District employees knew their first allegiance was to their patrons rather than Park District supervisors. Both hiring and promotion were the result of political pull. You could get ahead not by merit but rather by doing a good job on Election Day. Some Park District employees worked hard, but they could only partially make up for those who didn't feel they had to do their best.

Which parks received the most attention was also a matter of politics. People flocked to the well-maintained North Side lakefront, causing traffic congestion and overcrowding, while South Siders found few reasons to go near the undeveloped Burnham Park. On the West Side, very few people visited the aging Garfield Park Conservatory. Lack of funding saw large numbers of flowers freeze to death in poorly-heated and unrepaired sections of the structure.

No one at the top in the Chicago Park District seemed to believe the problems had solutions.

In early 1993, however, Mayor Daley appointed Forrest Claypool, known as a "go-to guy," general superintendent of the Park District, and things

THE BEAUTY OF THE CHICAGO WILDERNESS

FRANK LLOYD WRIGHT ON THE CHICAGO PARK SYSTEM

"The most beautiful city left in the modern world"? In the question and answer period of his 1939 London Lectures, Frank Lloyd Wright explained his statement:

First of all because it has a generous park system, the greatest on earth. You may drive the whole day without going away from the boulevard and park system of Chicago. And the parks are as well looked after as your own London parks, which is very well indeed. Another reason is that, thanks to an architect, Daniel Burnham, Chicago seems to be the only city in our States to have discovered its own waterfront. Moreover, to a greater extent than any other city it has a life of its own.

began to change. At the mayor's request, he started by clearing out many employees whom he felt were not delivering. He worked, at the same time, to revitalize the system's programs and even create new parks.

Under Claypool's guidance, the district began to rediscover its heritage, and recapture the greatness of the parks of the past.

To this day, many older Chicagoans speak with warm nostalgia of their local parks, telling how as children they had played in them, how they and their families had slept there on hot nights.

In the first half of the twentieth century, visitors and newcomers to the city wrote to those they left behind, sending penny postcards that had views of the city's parks. These scenes represented the Chicago they held dearest and of which they were the most proud.

The early parks of which Chicagoans were rightfully proud owe much of their success to a man named Jans Jensen. In 1905, Jensen was appointed general superintendent and chief landscape architect for the Chicago Park District. He both restored parks that had already begun to deteriorate and completed many unfinished projects in the newer ones.

One of his first efforts was Humboldt Park, a large expanse on the West Side. There, experimentation led him to evolve Prairie Style landscape design, which brought the wilderness back to the city some 90 years ago and is being replicated today.

For 20 years, Jensen worked to develop and improve the system, using innovation and imagination to create parks like no others in the world.

137

This was the park heritage of which so many have spoken—the heritage that Chicago has finally begun to restore.

The restoration that began in the early 1990s has been noted by local and national critics alike. *Crain's Chicago Business* reported, "Bottom line, the apparent turnaround of the Chicago Park District is for real—even astonishing." A *USA Today* article commented that cities such as Chicago with the most successful park systems "have strong leadership, strong public support and an entrepreneurial system."

One organization in particular has contributed greatly to the success of Chicago's parks. It is difficult to appreciate fully the ongoing vigilance and vision of the Friends of the Parks. The group is a volunteer organization that researches, consults, informs, lobbies and, when necessary, litigates on behalf of the public who use the parks.

Here is how the parks are retrieving their great heritage and purpose:

1. A Renewed Vision

Parks have one real purpose: to enrich the lives of the public. They provide individuals with opportunities to enjoy leisure activities and appreciate natural beauty. And in so doing, they enhance the livability of the city as a whole.

IN THE DETAILS: DREW BECHER

A new key player in the revitalization of the Park District is its chief of staff, Drew Becher. He is a former assistant to Mayor Daley, and has been in the center of Chicago's tree and flower efforts since starting as an unpaid intern in the city's Office of General Services in 1994. He has a bachelor's degree in urban planning from the University of Cincinnati and a master's degree in the same field from DePaul University.

The first project on which he was engaged was the beautification of the city's malls and plazas. It was a good place for Chicago and for him to start: many seat-of-the-pants ideas that were successful in that program are now at work in major projects across the city.

"This beautification thing is very strong," Becher says. "But know this: It is in the details. Get those right and it all works."

Without a clear sense of purpose, parks cannot work. If they are not designed to benefit the people, the community will reject them. And without their support, parks are either neglected or, worse, exploited.

In Chicago, this all-important vision was woefully lacking for almost half a century. Local parks became political tools instead of neighborhood front lawns. For several decades, park jobs were given out almost exclusively on the basis of political patronage. For six years in the 1980s, the Park District operated under a court order that forced it to deal with the racial inequities it had let fester within the system.

The Friends of the Parks realized that a true vision was lacking and sought to get the Park District back on course. In the early 1990s, Chicago's new mayor Richard M. Daley responded by telling the newly appointed Claypool to perform his "surgical strike" against uncommitted Park District workers.

A *Chicago Tribune* editorial said of Claypool when he left the job, "[He received] generally high marks from community groups and innumerable parents with restless kids."

The present superintendent, David Doig, is also committed to developing parks that serve the public first and foremost. His first words in an interview for this book were:

> To me, the parks are the core living rooms of the city, space where the community functions, children play and society functions across racial, age and gender lines. They must be safe, attractive, inviting, welcoming places to recreate and experience leisure time.

The "core living room" concept for a neighborhood park is certainly a vision that would have made Olmsted happy.

2. The CitySpace Plan

The first step in the restoration of the city's parks was CitySpace, an idea funded by the Chicago Community Trust. Under this plan, all the open land in Chicago was cataloged. The Chicago Planning Commission, the Park District and the Cook County Forest Preserves worked in concert for four years to put this inventory together. The future got started by building on the record of the past.

Flowers and landscaping of the Museum Campus (Brook Collins/Chicago Park District)

The compilation showed not only that the city needed more parks, especially in areas recently changed from industrial to residential, but also that a surprising amount of open land was still available within the city.

Even more importantly, the agencies that compiled the list worked together for the first time. This coordination continued—the agencies are now involved with one another on other projects, such as adding trees and flowers to the Chicago landscape.Now, they are sharing the responsibility for creating new gardens, establishing new parks and restoring both the river and the lakefront.

The same people are also working together to restore Lake Calumet, redevelop brownfields (former industrial sites) and improve existing parks.

3. The Big Projects

Other chapters of this book tell of major efforts to develop Burnham Park, the Chicago River, the Grant Park Museum Campus, Millennium Park and the Peggy Notebaert Nature Museum. The Chicago Park District is deeply involved in each of these projects, and has assumed a leadership role in planning, executing and maintaining many of them.

4. New Paths to Safety

For 30 to 40 years, perhaps longer, many Chicago parks have been unsafe, especially after sunset. As a result, Chicagoans have avoided them. Now, the Park District is finally addressing the problem.

"Creating places where people feel safe is not about more police," Chicago Park District superintendent David Doig said. "It's about creating an environment through physical planning. First of all, it is about having more people come out because they are not as isolated. You do that through fencing and lighting."

Potawatomi Park in the Rogers Park neighborhood is one proof of the program's success. The park has been renovated to add fencing and a dozen sets of large, bright lights shining down on it. Now, on warm evenings, kids and families picnic, play soccer or just stand around and talk in large groups into the late hours.

Neighbors believe the lights have made not only the park but also the nearby streets safer.

Fences help as much as the lights do to warn off would-be troublemakers. Both these additions have been made to parks throughout the city.

5. Restoration and Renovation

In the mid-1990s, the Chicago Park District quickly initiated two major projects to address issues that needed immediate attention. It arranged for the renovation of the deteriorating Garfield Park Conservatory, and made plans to restore a number of the city's most neglected parks.

The Garfield Park Conservatory, one of the largest indoor gardens in the country, is located in the middle of the West Side of the city, where residents of many other neighborhoods fear to tread. Its physical condition was so bad that large numbers of flowers were freezing over the winter.

The Park District took the attitude, "Rebuild it and they will come."

The Garfield Park Conservatory Alliance, a public/private partnership, was formed. The group's purpose is to obtain funding and perform planning and outreach services for the conservatory. It is now being restored

*Gold Dome
pavilion at
Garfield Park
(Brook Collins/
Chicago Park
District)*

through a $20 million Alliance effort. The children's garden has been completed, safety measures have been put in place, and free trolleys take people back and forth to the Loop.

As the trolley wends it way through the streets painted with images of the conservatory, it also serves as a colorful advertisement for the gardens.

In the second of their two emergency projects, park administrators have targeted an initial ten parks for major restoration. These include Humboldt and Columbus parks on the West Side.

Humboldt Park, in the middle of a Hispanic neighborhood in the center of the city, is enormous. In 1998 and 1999, the Chicago Park District performed a long-needed upgrading of the park. The work included an ecological rehabilitation, restoring natural habitats and improving the water quality in its Jens Jensen Prairie River and extensive lagoons. Landscape designers also created an imaginative Nature Walk with interpretative signs and brochures.

A local resident who drives daily through Columbus Park on the Far West Side, spoke of watching the transformation there.

"It had ceased being a park," he said. "I witnessed it going down over the past 25 years.

"Columbus just was no longer a park in my eyes. Rather it was a place for weeds to grow and where people discarded their garbage. Suddenly, I started seeing the grass being mowed and the trash being cleaned up. I watched day by day as workers constructed two new fountains.

Humboldt Park field house (Chicago Park District)

"Trees and flowers, lots of them, were planted. I saw people, not just park employees, picking up litter. I like fishing and learned the water there was now clean enough to fish in. Columbus is a park again and, I think, incredibly beautiful."

6. New Parks

In his book *Inside City Parks* (Urban Land Institute, 2000), Peter Harnik evaluated park acreage per capita in 25 major metropolitan areas, using a formula that excluded lakeshore parks. Chicago trailed all other evaluated cities except Miami.

One can quibble with Harnik's failure to see that the lakefront serves neighborhoods, but the need for more acreage is apparent. Fortunately, the Park District now has plans to acquire additional land, almost any way that it can. So far it has been busy:

- The first new park, Senka, opened in 1998, and was built over a former railway yard.

- The second and much larger park, also utilizes a former industrial site. This location on the South Shore had been home to South Works Steel Mills. It will serve both a recreational and an historical park that will honor the steel industry in Chicago, the employees who labored there and the strikers killed in the Labor Day Massacre of 1937.

- Another new project is the Ping Tom Memorial Park in Chinatown at 300 West 19th Street along the river, described in Chapter Two.

- Clark Park on the North Branch features a canoe and kayak launch.

- Canal Origins Park covers only three acres, but it is historically significant as an anchor end of the Illinois and Michigan Canal Corridor. This was a joint project with the State of Illinois.

The Park District is working to acquire land in subdivisions and areas of the city that have been transformed in recent years from industrial to residential. Also, builders are now being required to allot land for green space around such residential developments.

7. NeighborSpace

According to the CitySpace Plan survey, available open space in the city includes school land as well as tax delinquent and abandoned property. These sites have been investigated and many of them designated for parks or park-development sites.

Some West and South Side lots have already been turned over to the community for growing gardens or to the Park District for developing parks.

8. More Trees

How has the Chicago Park District joined in the campaign to add hundreds of thousands more trees to the city?

- By inserting trees in abundance when building new parks or renovating old ones.
- By planting them around buildings and the perimeters of parks;
- By replacing trees that have died;
- By making double rows of trees;
- By using trees to create canopies with their branches.

9. The Return of the Wilderness

One of the most worthy and precious parts of the Chicago Park District's heritage is the commitment of early Park District general superintendent and landscape architect Jens Jensen to returning the prairie to Chicago.

In the 1920s, Jensen's imaginative hand left a lasting imprint on the city. He was more than half a century ahead of his time in creating stunningly beautiful parks by re-introducing native plants, tallgrasses and flowers

"THE FLOWER BEDS ARE [NOW] ACTUALLY SUBTLE"

The Chicago Park System is "exhibiting a whole new planting sensitivity," commented Alison James, a resident of the city who was born in England and fell in love with the ubiquitous flower gardens she experienced there.

"Park District gardens used to very unsophisticated," she said. "They basically were examples of paint-by-number with flowers. If you want to see the difference, look now at the field of flowers just north of the main entrance to Lincoln Park Zoo. Instead of repetitious rows of gaudy, inappropriate annuals, the flower beds are [now] actually subtle."

CHICAGO'S PARKS: WAYS IN WHICH THEY'RE COMING BACK STRONG

The most dramatic examples of his efforts include his "Prairie Rivers" in both Humboldt and Washington parks, as well as his wetland in Gompers Park.

It was in Humboldt that he first extended a park's existing lagoon into a long, meandering Prairie River. Inspired by natural prairie rivers he traversed in the West and Midwest, he designed hidden water sources that supply two brooks that feed the river.

In 1998 and 1999, the Chicago Park District studied Jensen's pioneering ideas in parks such as Humboldt, Washington and Gompers and began using them to restore habitats and rehabilitate the shoreline.

The Park District issued a Nature Chicago brochure and a map that guide visitors to the wilderness areas that have been restored and developed in neighborhood parks.

10. A New Focus on Gardens

The Chicago Park District has become more aware of how theme gardens can serve both nearby citizens and the whole city.

The Park District has published a multi-color folder to celebrate the gardens of Chicago. One side opens into a poster (17 by 24 inches) of the Spirit of Music Garden at 601 South Michigan Avenue in Grant Park.

On the reverse side, nine panels show off the new looks of Lincoln Park Conservatory, the Jackson Park Osaka Garden, the Grant Park Cancer Survivors Garden, the Columbus Park waterfall, Humboldt Park, the South Shore Cultural Center, the Jackson Park Perennial Garden, the Washington Park Perennial Garden and Garfield Park.

The CHICAGO Skyline

Chicago . . . grew up from the savory of its neighborhoods to some of the best high-rise architecture in the world.

NORMAN MAILER, *MIAMI AND THE SIEGE OF CHICAGO*

Here is a conversation starter in Chicago. "From what point can you get the best view of the city's skyline?"

City of Chicago/Peter J. Schulz

City of Chicago/Peter J. Schulz

Chicago—hit's a frontier town.

Captain George Wellington Streeter

City of Chicago/Peter J. Schulz

[Chicago] gives a marvelous sense of space. It is the wideness of the Lake that does it: every New Yorker must look with envy and admiration at the great expanse of water-front, so that the whole city is open on one side.

Christopher Morley, *Old Loopy*

If the world has been my oyster, Chicago has been my cocktail sauce.

Columnist Louella Parsons

Chicago . . . the ultimate American city.

Andrew Neil, *The Economist,* 1980

A city which offers free play for prairie energy.

H. L. Mencken

▌The CHICAGO River

Most of America's great rivers have been carved by the slow forces of nature. But the profile of the Chicago River, as striking as any of the world's waterways, was wrought largely by human device. Its flow was determined by engineers, and its canyon walls designed by architects. Yet its splendor is real and its sheer majesty has become one of the city's great natural resources.

JAY PRIDMORE, *A VIEW FROM THE RIVER*

The Early River

Before fur traders and white settlers built log cabins and a fort in the area, the Chicago River was a slow-moving stream that constantly changed its path as it flowed through the prairie. Now the river is tamed and confined to narrow channels that are bordered by urban roads, buildings, parks and gardens.

Isabel S. Abrams,
The Nature of Chicago

A Place in History

The shortest of all strategic rivers, it unlocked the continent.

Harry Hansen, *The Chicago*

City of Chicago/Peter J. Schulz

© 1999 Dennis McClendon/Chicago CartoGraphics

An Historical Viewpoint

The best harbor on Lake Michigan . . . and the worst harbor and smallest river any great commercial city ever lived on.

Caroline Kirkland, "Chicago in 1856," *Putnam's Magazine*

A 1900 Commentary

Twas th' prettiest river f'r to look at that ye'll iver see.

Finley Peter Dunne's Bridgeport bartender, Mr. Dooley

City of Chicago/Javet M. Kimble

The Bend in the River

The Potawatomi Indians who lived near the stream had a keen appreciation of its geographic importance, so they called it Rora, a term meaning "confluence."

David M. Solzman, *The Chicago River*

The Excitement of the River

I am the mist,
Back of the thing you seek.
My arms are long,
Long as the reach of time
and space.

Carl Sandburg, *Chicago Poems*

© 1997 Dennis McClendon/Chicago CartoGraphics

▮The BIRDS

Bird of the wilderness,
Blythesome and cumberless . . .

JAMES HOGG, "THE SKYLARK"

The photos in this section were taken in the Chicago area by Jerry Garden, a former professional photographer and past president of the Chicago Audubon Society. He is now in charge of land management for the Emily Oaks Nature Center, 4650 Brummel Street, Skokie. The center includes a wooded area and a pond, and hosts birding activities on selected Saturdays. Similar activities are also offered by other nature centers in the area.

Jerry Garden

Great Blue Heron
The largest member of the heron family, the great blue heron departs from its relatives' staple diet of fish and other aquatic animals and moves inland to feed on rodents and gophers as well. It is stately and elegant—especially in flight. Fortunately for bird-lovers, it is fairly common throughout the Midwest.

Red-Tailed Hawk

This predator is a common, year-round resident of the Chicago Wilderness. It can often be seen soaring overhead or sitting on a post along the highway. It once bore the nickname "hen hawk," because people believed that it preyed on chickens. That reputation was largely undeserved—and it has faded as open chicken yards have become much less common.

Jerry Garden

American Bittern

As this photograph indicates, the American bittern is an expert at concealment. It is so clever that Thoreau called it "the genius of the bog." No one ever confused its throat-clearing song, however, with that of a warbler or nightingale. Though hard to spot, somewhat rare and a migrant, it can sometimes be discovered in marshes such as those in the Goose Lake Prairie State Park.

Jerry Garden

Yellow Warbler

One of the talents that a birder develops is the ability to see (and photograph) small birds that others can only hear. The sharp-eyed birder's reward is captured in this photo.

Jerry Garden

Jerry Garden

Black-Capped Chickadee

Distinctly a bird of the woods, this little bit of fluff is also known to birders as the black-capped titmouse. It stays around the Chicago area in the winter and can be seen frolicking in trees during the heaviest of snows and the worst of weather. Its call is the last syllable of its name.

Jerry Garden

House Wren

House wrens have earned the reputation of being eccentric little characters, often choosing to live around human beings and selecting items such as discarded hats and boxes in which to build their nests. In this picture, the friendly little bird looks like it is squawking at something or someone—and it probably is.

Jerry Garden

Brown Thrasher

This bird, with beautiful, rusty-brown feathers, is noted for its speckled breast. Its name comes from the movements of its tail when it is excited. Some intrusive people have discovered that the thrasher is capable of getting in a person's face—tail and all—if they insist on looking too closely at its nestlings.

Jerry Garden

Northern Cardinal
This bird is an exotic, resplendent red. It is common throughout the Chicago Wilderness, but delights and excites people whenever it is spotted. Area residents who have a family of cardinals on their block or in their yard consider themselves fortunate. Cardinals are fast-moving, busy and always on the go.

Jerry Garden

Yellow-Bellied Sapsucker
This bird has a cute name, a beautiful coat and a bad habit. Although a member of the woodpecker family, it does not tap into trees to get insects like its relatives. It bores deeper than they do, ignoring their prey in order to reach the tree's sap. In the course of its pursuit, the yellow-bellied sapsucker often causes serious damage to trees.

Jerry Garden

American Coot
The old saying is, "If it looks like a duck, swims like a duck and walks like a duck, it must be a duck." Well, the coot does most of these things, but it is not a duck. It is a member of the rail family and its feet are not webbed. The American coot is fairly common in the Chicago Wilderness, but is spotted only rarely along the Lake Michigan shoreline. It is usually found in shallow lakes and sloughs.

▌The FLOWERS of the Tallgrass Prairies

In our modern world with its artificiality, complexity and instability,
wild flowers can provide us with places to go for peace and solitude.
For this alone, prairies should be preserved and cherished.

BIOLOGIST ROBERT F. BETZ

These photos of prairie and dune plants are the work of the late Torkel Korling and are used here through the graciousness of Diane Korling. In them, the talents of the photographer have effectively captured the beauty of both individual species and the community of plants that surrounds them.

Torkel Korling

Shooting Star
The Roman historian Pliny called the primrose *Dodecatheon*, which means "12 gods." Linnaeus, who first categorized the plant world, applied that Latin name to the prairie plant shooting star, which is in the primrose family.

Torkel Korling

Torkel Korling

Kalm's Saint John's Wort

To protect themselves from the forces of evil, people in the Middle Ages hung sprigs of Saint John's wort on their doors for Midsummer Night's Day, the pagan feast day which occurs on the summer solstice. Saint John's wort is still used as an herbal medicine.

Big Bluestem

This tall and majestic prairie grass is often indistinguishable from other grasses of the prairie until late in the season. It then develops its characteristic "turkey foot" seed heads, so called because they are shaped like a bird's feet.

Butterfly Weed
The butterfly weed's flowers are beautiful and distinctive. It is found in habitats that include sandy black-oak forests, dry prairies and dune areas.

Torkel Korling

Fringed Gentian
According to one historian, the gentian plants received their name from Gentius, a king of the second century BC. He reportedly used them as a medicine against the plague. The fringed gentian has become more rare in the Midwest than it was a half-century ago.

Torkel Korling

Torkel Korling

Rattlesnake Master
Rattlesnake master helps botanists identify an area as a prairie remnant, as it is one of the most common plants in such a habitat. It can also be found in both wet and mesic prairies.

Saw-Tooth Sunflower

The saw-toothed sunflower belongs to the scientific genus *Helianthus,* which is Greek for "sunflower." To the ancient Greeks, the term described a flower whose face always pointed towards the sun. Today, we apply the name to this New World plant whose petals resemble the sun's rays. The saw-tooth sunflower is found in prairies throughout the Midwest, even in degraded prairies.

Torkel Korling

Wild Quinine

This plant, along with shooting star and rattlesnake master, is one of the true prairie plants. It is commonly found in black soil prairies and level sand prairies

Torkel Korling

Torkel Korling

Prairie Blazing Star

This charming plant, which begins to bloom in the middle of July, is restricted to prairie remnants. Other local species of blazing star are named rough, cylindrical, dotted and marsh blazing star.

█CHICAGO Botanic Garden

At the Chicago Botanic Garden, native prairies and climbing roses provide animate links connecting the romantic past with the promise of the future.

A *GARDEN WALK*, PUBLISHED BY THE WOMAN'S BOARD

The Rose Garden

With the Rose Petal Fountain as their centerpiece, roses cover three acres of the Botanic Garden. The 160 varieties include shrub, antique and heirloom roses and are arranged for viewing in order from the palest to the deepest colors.

Chicago Botanic Garden/Cliff Zenor

The Sensory Garden

A variety of fragrances and textures highlights this unusual garden. It was developed especially for the enjoyment of the visually impaired, but delights all visitors.

The Suzanne S. Dixon Prairie

Located on a peninsula jutting out into the lagoon, this special place is in actuality six distinct prairies: mesic prairie, bur oak savanna, wet prairie, fen, gravel hill prairie and sand prairie. These habitats restore to this patch of land the colorful, dramatic beauty that characterized the area a century and a half ago.

The Japanese Garden
The arched bridge leads to Sansho-En, the Garden of Three Islands. Completed in 1982 as a stroll garden, it expresses the Zen Buddhist belief in self-examination and enlightenment. In the foreground is a Yukimi (snow-viewing lantern).

The English Walled Garden
This elegant, restrained area, south of the Rose Garden, contains five outdoor "rooms." Each offers the visitor a style typical of English gardening. As is traditional in such gardens, the brick walls partially protect the flowers and other plants from the elements.

Chicago Botanic Garden/Joanne Dahlberg

Fall Colors

Hal Borland called a single tree in full color "a dancing tongue of flame to warm the heart."

The Circle Garden

In spring, the Circle Garden celebrates youth and renewal with tulips and other bright flowers—and by attracting visitors that include small children.

A Winter Scene

The flowers are all gone or snuggled away in the greenhouses, but beauty has not abandoned the landscape of the Chicago Botanic Garden. A booklet, *A Portrait of a Garden,* notes that, in winter, "The pleasures of the place are more subtle.... For many horticulturists and visitors, the frozen months are when the imagination is the richest and the most vivid gardens are planned."

Chicago Botanic Garden/Robert C. V. Lieberman

Chicago Botanic Garden

▮ The MORTON Arboretum

*Our goal is to encourage the planting and conservation of trees
and other plants for a greener, healthier and more beautiful world.*

MORTON ARBORETUM BROCHURE

*The land itself reads well. . . . I have offered my interpretations, in the hope that you
will put the book down and go eagerly out, to examine for yourself the original manu-
script which starts at your doorstep.*

Naturalist May Theilgaard Watts, founder of Arboretum's education program

Morton Arboretum

*Acts of creation are ordinarily
reserved for gods and poets. To
plant a pine, one need only own
a shovel.*

Conservationist Aldo Leopold

Morton Arboretum

The land ethic simply enlarges the boundaries of the community to include soils, waters, plants, and animals, or collectively: the land.

Conservationist Aldo Leopold

To exist as a nation, to prosper as a state, and to live as a people, we must have trees.

President Theodore Roosevelt

The best friend on earth of man is the tree. When we use the tree respectfully and economically, we have one of the greatest resources of the earth.

Architect Frank Lloyd Wright

▌CHICAGO'S Parks

Chicago . . . has a generous park system, the greatest on earth.

FRANK LLOYD WRIGHT, 1939

An Apt Analogy
Parks of a city have been compared with the lungs of a person.

Wacker's Manual
of the Plan of
Chicago, 1911

Land Use by the Park District
Chicago makes the most of what it has, intensively managing and using virtually every inch of land, unlike most other cities that have large tracts of undeveloped properties.

Peter Harnik, *Inside City Parks,* 2000

The Parks as Opportunity

City people need to connect with nature and, fortunately, Chicago abounds in green havens for all to enjoy. You will find parks with meadows, groves of trees, lagoons and flowerbeds in every sector of the city.

Isabel S. Abrams, *The Nature of Chicago*

Grant Park

This park of 205 acres will be the most beautiful and most serviceable park contiguous to the business district of any city in the world.

Report to the South Park Commissioners, February 28, 1908

Armour Square Park Flowers

Armour Square, 3900 South Shield Avenue, is one of the city's "immigrant parks." It was created to help ease foreigners into American life. Flowers, such as these snapdragons, welcome area residents today.

Gompers Park Wetland

During the 1950s the northwest side of Gompers Park, then a wetland, was filled in to make mowing easier. In the late 1990s, however, the Park District dredged the area and let river water flow into the depression it created. Hundreds of children and other volunteers then put in 4,000 specially selected plants to restore a wet meadow habitat.

Ten Lesser-Known LANDMARKS

The following selections and their descriptions were compiled with help from the staff of the Commission on Chicago Landmarks. A complete listing of all buildings and districts designated as official Chicago landmarks, complete with photos, can be seen on the commission's web site: www.ci.chi.il.us/Landmarks/List.html.

Commission on Chicago Landmarks

The American School of Correspondence
850 East 58th Street
Built: 1906–7
Architect: Pond and Pond

Considered a masterpiece of Arts & Crafts–style design, this building was constructed as the headquarters for a mail-order school. Special features include extraordinary brickwork and extensive decorative details.

Bob Thall/Commission on Chicago Landmarks

The Powhatan Apartments
4950 South Chicago Beach Drive
Built: 1927–29
Architects: Robert DeGolyer and Charles Morgan

The façade of this 22-story apartment highrise reflects the influential streamlined design of Eliel Saarinen's entry in the 1922 Tribune Competition. The building is named for a famous Algonquin chief, and features ornamental terra cotta panels depicting scenes from the lives of Native Americans.

The Fisher Studio Houses
1209 North State Parkway
Built: 1936
Architect: Andrew Rebori, with Edgar Miller

This residential complex is a rare example of the *Art Moderne* style of architecture. The building has 12 units with a common courtyard. Artist Edgar Miller designed its handcrafted ornamentation.

Commission on Chicago Landmarks

Four Houses by Frederick Schock
5749 & 5804 West Race Avenue; 5804 & 5810 West Midway Park
Built: 1886–92
Architect: Frederick R. Schock

Schock, a local architect, designed these Queen Anne– and Shingle-style homes and helped set the tone for the residential development of Austin in the 1880s and 1890s, before the area was annexed by Chicago.

Bob Thall/Commission on Chicago Landmarks

Bob Thall/Commission on Chicago Landmarks

Bob Thall/Commission on Chicago Landmarks

Bob Thall/Commission on Chicago Landmarks

The Humboldt Park Boathouse Pavilion

1301 North Humboldt Boulevard
Built: 1906–7
Architect: Richard E. Schmidt,
Garden & Martin, with Jens Jensen

Jens Jensen, during his years as Chicago Park District general superintendent, brought the Prairie Style of architecture to bear on park building construction. With this design, architect Hugh Garden developed a progressive style of architecture that still influences modern building.

Schurz High School

3601 North Milwaukee Avenue
Built: 1910
Architect: Dwight H. Perkins

This large school building is an imaginative combination of two different schools of architecture. The strong vertical piers are characteristic of the Chicago School, while the overhanging roof and strong geometric forms typify Prairie School architecture. Perkins designed this and other buildings for the Chicago Board of Education from 1905 to 1910.

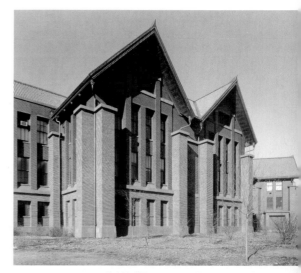

The Brewster Apartments

2800 North Pine Grove Avenue
Built: 1893
Architects: Enoch Hill Turnock

Once upon a time and with some justification, this structure was known as the "Lincoln Park Palace." Today, it is on the "Great Interiors" and "Innovative Housing" architectural tours of the city. It features a massive skylight, bridge walkways paved with glass blocks, elevator cages, cast-iron stairs and an exceptionally light and airy interior construction.

The Reebie Storage Warehouse
2325–2333 North Clark Street
Built: 1921–22
Architect: George Kingsley, with Fritz Albert

This eye-catching building is one of the most pleasing and respected examples of pure Egyptian Revival commercial architecture in the country. It is celebrated for its accurate use of ancient Egyptian imagery and hieroglyphics. Fritz Albert crafted the colorful terra cotta ornamentation.

Bob Thall/Commission on Chicago Landmarks

Commission on Chicago Landmarks

The Bachman House
1244 West Carmen Avenue
Built: 1947–48
Architect: Bruce Goff

Goff created a neighborhood sensation and a national attraction by remodeling a modest wood house into this home and studio for recording engineer Myron Bachman. In addition to changing the windows dramatically, the inimitable architect also added the brick and aluminum. Much of Goff's work was done in Oklahoma, but he also maintained a practice in Chicago during the 1930s and 1940s.

Bob Thall/Commission on Chicago Landmarks

The Colvin House
5940 North Sheridan Road
Built: 1909
Architect: George W. Maher

Maher began his career working on residential designs under Frank Lloyd Wright. This building's bold rectangular shape, broad-hipped roof and dominant central entrance embody the styles of both men.

▮The CHILDREN

This section celebrates Chicago's most beautiful asset, its children—as seen by the photographers of CITY 2000. The CITY 2000 project, sponsored by the Comer Foundation and directed by Richard Cahan, documented everyday life in Chicago in the year 2000. The entire collection—over 10,000 images—can be found at the University of Illinois at Chicago, in the Special Collections Department of the Richard J. Daley library.

Steve Matteo/CITY 2000

Steve Matteo
Gage Park, May 6

Balter Gonzalez, age four, attacks an ice cream sundae in Gertie's Own Ice Cream parlor, 5858 South Kedzie Avenue.

Wes Pope
Hyde Park, March 20

Naomi Itskoff, five, wears a wary look as Elmo (Rabbi Doug Sagal) leads the reading of the Megallah during Purim at K.A.M. Isaiah Israel Congregation.

Wes Pope
Eden Green, March 2

Robert "B. J." Samuels receives a kiss from his grandmother, Joyce Samuels, on his way home from DuBois Elementary School

Wes Pope
Altgeld Gardens, February 7

Dominique Martin, 11, watches as art therapist David Hawkins gives a painting lesson at the Altgeld Health Clinic.

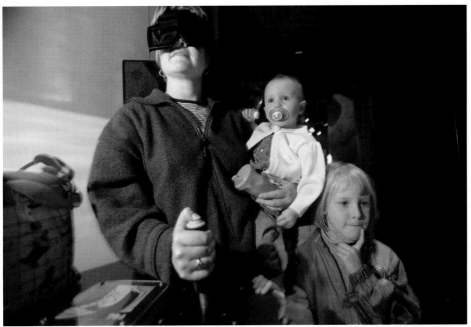

Wes Pope
River North, April 13

A bottle in one hand and a controller in the other, mother of two Rene Struck plays Hercules in the Underworld at DisneyQuest. Her children are Paige, 20 months, and Lauren, five.

Leah Missbach
Streeterville, February 29

August Fuller, age two, who is with his mother on field service work for the Jehovah's Witnesses, passes out leaflets.

Yvette Marie Dostatni
Archer Heights, April 30

Monica Coloa, flower girl for the Ricardo and Margarita Reyes wedding, has her hair prepared by her mother for picture taking at Raphael Photo, 4161 South Archer Avenue.

Scott Strazzante/CITY 2000

Scott Strazzante

Harbor Point Estates, Hegewisch, April 22

Cheered on by her dog, Champ, three-year-old Stephanie Johnson spins a hula-hoop in the lone mobile home park at the Chicago city limits.

Zbigniew Bzdak

O'Hare, April 22

Two children celebrate Lazarus Saturday, a Serbian Orthodox holiday, with the traditional palms and pussy willows in Holy Resurrection Serbian Orthodox Cathedral.

Zbigniew Bzdak/CITY 2000

Alyce Henson/CITY 2000

Alyce Henson
River West, February 6

Youngsters play and perform at the Lake Shore Academy of Artistic Gymnastics, 937 Chestnut Street.

Robert A. Davis/CITY 2000

Robert A. Davis
East Rogers Park, February 6

As their parents welcome in the Tibetan New Year (2127) with chanted prayers and offerings, young traders negotiate Pokémon card deals at the Tibetan Cultural Center, 5200 North Sheridan Road.

Pete Barreras/CITY 2000

Pete Barreras
Burnside, March 23

Boys on the left and girls on the right at Harold Washington Elementary School. The students' family portraits are on the wall in the background.

15. Public Gardens of the CHICAGO AREA: TEN MEANINGFUL, WHIMSICAL AND BEAUTIFUL ONES

A garden is a lovesome thing . . .

—THOMAS EDWARD BROWN

Long ago, monarchs of the world began to surround themselves with magnificent gardens, such as the awe-inspiring Hanging Gardens of Babylon or the extensive and well-manicured gardens at Versailles.

Today, in the Chicago Wilderness region and elsewhere, extraordinarily beautiful gardens also grow. They belong neither to the kings nor to the powerful, but to the public.

From the expansive plots of the Chicago Botanic Garden and Chicago Park District to the smallest neighborhood patch, gardens in this area are blossoming with new imagination and beauty.

This is all understandable because just as the gardens belong to the people, so the public is now volunteering to become a part of them.

"How deeply seated in the human heart," Alexander Smith has said, "is the liking for gardens and gardening!"

As a result of this growing interest, the gardens of today have been given a broader mission. They are being designed with purpose far beyond the satisfaction of self, beyond even beauty for beauty's sake. Their flowers are being used to call our attention to specific groups or issues—little children, grandmothers, those with disabilities, peace, hope, friendship, the local community and international brotherhood.

The gardens also say something about those who designed, planted or maintain them. Every designed garden was created by a designer; before every pruned plant, there was a pruner; and behind every cared-for flower is a care-giving person.

And with every public garden, there are staff and volunteers.

The following public gardens have been selected not simply for how they look, but also for the messages they were designed to convey. In addition, they were chosen to honor the tens of thousands of private gardens which people have planted on their own.

1. The Buehler Enabling Garden

> *The Chicago Botanic Garden: Lake Cook Road in Glencoe, one half mile east of the Edens Expressway.*

The sign outside the Buehler Enabling Garden reads, "Gardening for people of all abilities."

This showcase garden features special landscaping, flowers, tools and techniques that allow seniors and those with disabilities to enjoy "both the physical and emotional benefits of gardening," according to press material issued by the Chicago Botanic Garden.

Individuals with arthritis or muscular dystrophy, or those who have had a stroke can learn how to hoe, weed, plant and tend flowers even though their hands or bodies have limited strength or use. The garden is a demonstration area in which techniques are taught and counseling is given:

- Staff members have taken special training in or are currently studying a new field in medicine, horticultural therapy.

- The layout of this garden allows people in wheelchairs to work with flowers growing in containers at their level of reach.

Buehler Enabling Garden (Chicago Botanic Garden/ William Biderbost)

- Hanging baskets of flowers in the garden can be lowered or raised with pulleys.

- People with disabilities such as arthritis can use or purchase ergonomically-designed hoes, weeders, forks, cultivators and trowels. These each have a pistol grip to keep the wrist in a natural position and alleviate strain.

- Visitors are encouraged to touch many of the plants in the garden, as well as the water gently falling down two water walls.

The Chicago Botanic Garden first pioneered a "Learning Garden for the Disabled" in 1976. It was studied and imitated around the world. The Buehler Garden, which was dedicated in 1999, has dramatically upgraded the easy-access features developed in the earlier garden.

The garden is formal in setting, but informal in the pattern and choice of flowers. Three large, outdoor, ceiling-less "rooms" share walls of stone and brick. They include a gallery garden, a container or planter room and an overlook area. They offer planting beds lush with a great variety of flowers and plants that range from tall, exotic tropical roses to petite and friendly pansies.

The enabling garden is located next to the William Bacon Sr. Sensory Garden, which is considered complementary in purpose and mission to the enabling area.

2. The Elizabeth Morse Genius Children's Garden

> *Garfield Park Conservatory: 300 North Central Park Avenue, Chicago.*

The new Elizabeth Morse Genius Children's Garden at Garfield Park is, according to a Chicago Park District brochure, "Part garden, part exhibit

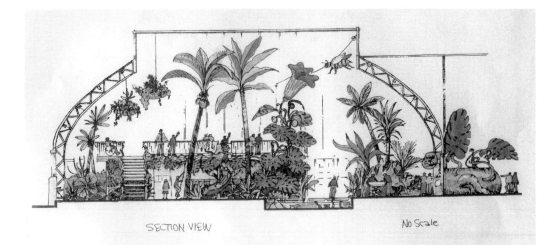

SECTION VIEW   No Scale

Design for the Children's Garden (Chicago Park District)

and part playground." No other children's garden anywhere in the United States, the Park District maintains, offers this combination of features.

This is an indoor garden in a large, two-level room in the Garfield Park Conservatory. Visitors enter through a tunnel made to look like a tree root. The area is full of a wide variety of real flowers as well as models of various others.

The garden is also a playground. Children can climb on a large pumpkin and ride a slide from one level of the garden to the other. A giant bee can be reeled in by a young visitor and used to "pollinate" a six-foot sunflower. A seven-foot seed demonstrates how something can be so seemingly dead and yet have potential life pulsing inside it.

The garden's "Plants Alive" exhibit affords a unique, multi-sensory environment to capture the imagination of the children while teaching them about the birth, growth and reproduction of plants

The Children's Garden is new, having been completed in August 2000. Attending the opening ceremonies was former Chicago alderman Leon Despres, 92 years of age at the time.

"I looked in the room and what I saw and heard were children giggling and screeching with delight," he said.

As a child in 1915 and 1916, he had gone with his parents to the three different conservatories that then existed in Washington Park.

"I was bored," he said. "I never did understand why they wanted me to go along with them. Someone at last has figured out how to involve little children in a flower garden."

Admission and parking for the conservatory are always free. There also is no charge for a trolley bus that goes back and forth to the conservatory from the Chicago Cultural Center and two Loop hotels.

3. The Osaka Garden

Jackson Park: on the Wooded Island, immediately south of the Museum of Science and Industry.

This garden bonds two sister cities, Chicago and Osaka, Japan. Each city has contributed to its development over the years, on a site where the Japanese government first constructed a pavilion for the 1893 World's Fair.

A traditional hill-style Japanese "stroll garden," it is made in the form of those developed in Japan during the Edo period (1615 to 1867 AD). A path leads the visitor from view to view, and the layout utilizes a venerable Japanese gardening technique called shakkei, or borrowed scenery. This makes use of various backgrounds of trees and vistas to frame what is in front of the viewer. As is traditional in such Japanese creations, there are rocks, water, a moon bridge and a pavilion with an Iromaya-style roof.

The garden was expanded several times and then rededicated in a ceremony on August 12, 2000.

The Wooded Island itself is closely identified with the late Clarence Darrow, known as "The Attorney for the Damned." It was his favorite place for relaxing and his ashes were scattered from the bridge leading to it. His admirers meet there in the spring to commemorate his work. This same island is also home to the Paul A. Douglas Nature Preserve.

4. Ravenswood Prairie Garden

A Lake View neighborhood garden: along Ravenswood Avenue, north of Belmont on the east bank of the railroad tracks.

An upper-level rider on the Union Pacific Railroad heading north through the city starts to see gardens at Belmont Avenue. The speed of the

train usually prevents him or her from identifying any species of plants there, but the passenger easily notices that there are flowers, trees and bushes rather than the rubbish and trash of the past.

The Osaka Garden at Jackson Park (Brook Collins/ Chicago Park District)

This is a distinct but, at the same time, representative Chicago neighborhood garden, an example of the city's GreenCorps program in action.

Like many other new gardens throughout Chicago, this one is the result of an alliance between local residents and the city. Two young women who lived in the condominium building facing the railroad tracks contemplated growing flowers along the railroad right of way, but lacked adequate training and funding to do it right. For example, they purchased bulbs to place in the ground, but then discovered it was the wrong season in which to plant them.

They learned that through the GreenCorps program they could each take a free six-week, part-time gardening course and even obtain funds to help pay for the project. The two of them did so, and then brought together other residents of the building to help with the planting.

The result is basically a prairie garden, with two non-prairie interlopers: lilac bushes and tomato plants.

Mayor Daley, passing this site, reportedly commented, "This is what railroad embankments should look like." He subsequently initiated a program for embankment beautification elsewhere in the city.

5. Richard & Annette Bloch Cancer Survivors Garden

*Grant Park: in the northeast corner of the park, west of
Lake Shore Drive.*

Gardens, which are manifestations of the life force, express birth, death and rebirth—a cycle that speaks of hope. Few generate such a thought as poignantly as this unique and beautiful site on Chicago's front lawn, Grant Park.

In 1996, Richard Bloch, a 21-year lung cancer survivor, donated $1 million to the Chicago Park District to build a garden that proclaims, "Cancer and death are not synonymous."

THE BEAUTY OF THE CHICAGO WILDERNESS

The Cancer Survivors Garden is further intended to give those diagnosed with cancer hope for a happy and productive life and to offer support to their families and friends.

It has three tiered "rooms," which symbolize stages of healing—recognition, support and wellness, and community celebration.

Roses, representing spring renewal, lead people to the Triumphal Arch. This structure was created from two 48-foot Corinthian columns, once part of the city's old Federal Office Building that had been designed in 1905 by Henry Ives Cobb and then demolished in 1966. The massive pieces were rescued for this purpose after having been used for a time as part of a retaining wall on Lake Michigan.

The arch leads to the first room, Acceptance Plaza, where pediatric oncology patients from four area hospitals have planted tulips and daffodils.

The Positive Mental Attitude Walk, lined with junipers and daylilies, has benches that offer a place to sit and talk with family and friends. 14 signs display inspirational messages.

The third room of the garden is called the Celebration Plaza. Connected to it is a butterfly garden that represents cancer survivors and their families reaching out to the community.

Each year, the Y-Me Breast Cancer Organization holds a candlelight vigil at the garden as part of its Race for the Cure event.

6. Ground Cover Garden

Morton Arboretum: 25 miles west of Chicago on the East-West Tollway. North off the tollway at the Route 53 exit.

Ground cover plants, which can be a significant part of any garden or landscaping effort, are those that range from one to four inches high.

These plants are not only attractive, but also quite useful. They can unify unrelated landscape elements, define or emphasize certain areas or features, soften harsh walls and embankments, and control erosion on slopes.

The selection of shrubs and plants available for creating ground cover is almost endless. Few gardeners can easily make imaginative and successful choices simply by picking through options available in pots or rows at a local nursery.

The Ground Cover Garden at the Morton Arboretum is appealing in itself and can help individuals make such decisions. It also has educated thousands of gardeners, students, landscape contractors and architects, teaching them to create more beautiful settings for the places where people live and work.

Recently renovated with new plantings and interpretation panels, the Ground Cover Garden offers more than 500 varieties of ground cover plants for sun and shade.

7. The Shakespeare Garden

The Northwestern University campus: on the east side of Sheridan Road in Evanston, just north of Garrett Theological Seminary.

The Shakespeare Garden is a formal, almost classical place to pause, enjoy nature, and read or contemplate.

It is old, having been founded in 1915 by the Garden Club of Evanston.

What is unique about this garden is that it features flowers, bushes and trees mentioned in the writings of Shakespeare. These include lavender, mint, marjoram, marigolds, daffodils, primroses and "lilies of all kinds, the flower deluxe being one," according to a plaque at the site.

A monument to the Bard quotes from *A Midsummer Night's Dream*:

> I know a bank where the wild thyme blows
> Where oxlips and the nodding violet grows
> Quite over-canopied with luscious woodbine
> With sweet musk-roses and with eglantine.

The Shakespeare Garden, approximately the size of a football field, has a bowered walk around the perimeter, with several places for sitting.

The Garden Club of Evanston maintains the garden, which was added to the National Registry of Historic Places in 1988.

8. Rockford, Illinois, Area Gardens

> *On the Rock River, 84 miles northwest of Chicago, just*
> *outside of the Chicago Wilderness.*

Long ago, Rockford chose the nickname "Forest City," because an early census showed 122 trees to the block. Today, it might better be called the "Garden City" or "Flower City"—it has so many public gardens, arboretums, orchards and natural areas that its Convention and Visitors Bureau put out a pamphlet, "Garden Spots in Illinois' Rockford area," to direct people to them.

These garden spots include:

- *The Klehm Arboretum and Botanic Garden.* In 1910, this 155-acre site was owned by landscaper William Lincoln Taylor, who liked to experiment with trees and other plants. Some of these experiments are now part of an extraordinary collection of gardens and "the Midwest's most vigorous evergreen collection."
- Rockford College's *Jane Addams International Peace Garden* at Fisher Chapel. Nobel laureate Addams was an alumna of the school.
- *Anderson Japanese Gardens,* acclaimed as "America's most authentic."
- *Sinnissippi Gardens, Greenhouse & Lagoon.* Adjacent to the 10-mile Rock River Recreation Path.
- *Severson Dells Environmental Education Center.* It offers 369 acres with an unusual 90% concentration of native flowers.

The guide pamphlet is available by contacting the Rockford Convention & Visitors Bureau, 211 North Main Street, Rockford IL 61101-1010.

9. Lilacia Park

> *Lemont, Illinois: West of Main Street, between Parkside*
> *and Maple Streets.*

Lemont's Lilacia Park is as special to people in the Chicago and DuPage/Will County area as its name. A surprising number of Chicago-area residents can correctly identify Lilacia as the name of this 8 1/2-acre garden in southwest suburban Lemont.

The best time to visit this garden park, designed by Jens Jensen, is during the annual spring lilac festival. The visitor will encounter lilac bushes of all colors, a great variety of plants and some 35,000 tulips. Later in the year, the garden offers prairie plants, perennial flowers and groves of both hardwood trees and firs.

10. Grandmother's Garden

*Lincoln Park: west of Stockton Drive, across from the Lincoln
Park Conservatory.*

The Grandmother's Garden in Lincoln Park is one of the oldest gardens in the Chicago area, dating from the early 1890s. Created by Carl Stromback, the park's head gardener during that era, it was created as a naturalist garden. According to a Park District fact sheet, this garden was intended to be a "profusion of flowers combined according to color and foliage."

Plants which are found in the garden include such perennials as asters, flocks, dianthus, coreopsis and aquilegia.

During the years of the intervening century the garden continued to contrast with the "French style" of the formal garden directly across Stockton Drive. The latter is arranged in set forms and conventional designs.

Everything about the garden—like a good grandmother—is meant to be friendly.

A statue of a sitting Shakespeare rests nearby, and is the source of the garden's second name—the Old English Garden.

▋ 16. The Forest PRESERVES:
THE CHICAGO AREA'S
WILDER SIDE

With the ever-increasing tempo of urban life, the true value of forest preserves lands lies with the future.

—REPORT OF THE COOK COUNTY FOREST PRESERVES, 1971

For the nature preserves in the Chicago Wilderness, the future is now.

The state's forest preserve districts, the first of which were created in 1915, have become caught up in the nature conservation and open space movement that is now sweeping this country, especially in the Midwest.

For the forest and other nature preserves this new awareness has meant large increases in the numbers of visitors and volunteers, and greater support for bond issues that fund such areas. This focus has fueled governments' desire to acquire more open space for forest preserves, even as undeveloped land decreases in availability.

It is the forest preserves' splendor, variety and beauty which are the attraction. People are starting to call the species of trees by their names, to recognize the birds by their calls and to identify the various glacial land formations. They volunteer to help seed tallgrass prairies, clean rivers and assist visitors. They have come to know which soil is best for certain plants and how to protest the destruction of wetlands.

The forest preserves, in turn, are reaching out as never before with newsletters, bird lists and web sites. The employees who operate and maintain them are receiving intense training in specific areas of conservation and land management.

Until recently, land was acquired for forest preserves and parks in several inefficient ways. Either a handful of believers attempted to snatch key parcels of land from the jaws of commercial or residential development, or preserves and parks were granted land through the occasional bequest. Now, the process is so sophisticated that the forest preserves, money in hand, are winning battles they would not even have thought to fight in the past.

Today, forest preserves are also acquiring land more purposefully than before. DuPage County, for example, set out to create continuous bands of open space along major waterways and between communities. Will County has developed a former quarry as a heron rookery and McHenry County has acquired a parcel because it supports a population of white lady's slipper orchids.

McHenry County has sites that include meadows, bogs, trail, fens and marshes that are not open to the public because the property contains rare or endangered plant or animal species which must be protected. (And because several of these properties require planning and development work to ensure the safety of the public.)

Waterway preserves are being supplemented by bike paths, interpretative centers and canoe launches such as one on the Nippersink Creek.

Here is a report on five Chicago-area forest preserve districts:

Cook County Forest Preserves

County population: 1990—5,105,067; 2000—5,376,741

One needs a map to begin to comprehend the enormity of these public lands. Much of the land follows the path of the Des Plaines River, from the north of the metropolitan area to south of it. To those speeding by in their cars, only the perimeter of the vast woods is visible.

The county's Forest Preserve District maintains 67,152 acres that include 137 major woods, 36 lakes and ponds, five nature centers and three swimming pools, plus golf courses, toboggan slides and miles of horse riding trails.

Unfortunately for Chicago, less than 5% of these acres are in the city. While the Cook County Forest Preserve District has become a partner in some park and river development going on in Chicago, officials there are asking them to increase their land ownership as well. The Forest Preserve argues that it has a cap on spending, and that few pristine lands remain available in the city.

In the spring of 2001, an investigation resulted in charges of mismanagement on the part of the Forest Preserve District. Consequently, $14 to $20 million were switched from the capital funds for land acquisition to the operating fund. Still, the property of the county forest preserves is impressive.

The Cook County Forest Preserves are the land on which sits Brookfield Zoo, the Chicago Botanic Garden and the Chicago Portage National Historic Site.

And not to be forgotten are the Cook County Forest Preserves' 2,200 picnic groves.

Will County Forest Preserves

County population: 1990—357,313; 2000—502,266

Of all the areas in the Chicago Wilderness, Will County best illustrates the new commitment to using nature to enhance human life. The county's recent record has been extraordinary:

1. In 1984, the federal government designated the pathway of the Illinois and Michigan Canal and the Chicago Outlet Valley as "The Illinois and Michigan National Heritage Corridor." Without question, Will County is at its heart. The Corridor's long, winding path through the area includes historic and often naturally wild strips of land full of special places. These are, according to Tony Hiss in the book *Prairie Passage,* "almost hidden in plain sight."

2. In 1996, President Clinton signed a bill to create the Midewin National Tallgrass Prairie on Will County land formerly used as the Joliet Arsenal. When fully realized, this will be the largest tallgrass

prairie east of the Mississippi River. With the help of federal funds, the work of expert prairie developers and the efforts of more than 600 volunteers, it promises to become a place of wonder and awe. Here bison and elk will once again roam.

3. In 1999, Will County voters passed a $70 million bond issue to enhance their forest preserves. For years, voters across the state and around the country had repeatedly rejected such bond proposals. But this time the vote was an astounding 57% to 43% in favor. These funds allow the county forest preserve district to spend $51 million to acquire additional land and $19 million to develop public access to the county's wetlands, forests and prairies. Lands already purchased as a result of the referendum include Sandridge Savanna Nature Preserve (152 acres), Spring Creek (151 acres), Forked Creek (155 acres) and Joliet Junction Trail (0.5 acres).

4. The Lake Renwick Heron Rookery was created in 1990 near Plainfield in Will County. For more information on this remarkable site, see the discussion in Chapter Eleven.

5. In 2000, quarry operator Material Service Corporation paid out $7 million in a settlement "for the alleged destruction of rare wetland habitats near Romeoville." The Forest Preserve District of Will County will get nearly $2 million of this, with almost all of the money going toward restoring prairie, wetlands and rare species habitats in sections of the 250-acre Lockport Prairie Nature Preserve.

DuPage County Forest Preserves

County population: 1990—781,666; 2000—904,161

Open land in DuPage has been gobbled up during the last 25 years at a pace matched by few other suburban areas in the United States. The work the county has done to maintain and expand its forest preserves is, therefore, vital to the future of the area as the clock of urban sprawl continues to tick.

In the early 1990s, DuPage had 23,000 acres of forest preserves. The property inventory at the turn of the century tallied 600 acres of lakes, 60 miles of rivers and streams and 80 miles of trails. The preserves employed 256 full-time, 32 part-time and 200 seasonal workers, and had a substantial budget of $175 million.

The big question is whether or not these figures are sufficient to meet the needs of the area's greatly expanded population. In 2015, the DuPage Forest Preserve District will celebrate its 100th birthday, and the population of the county will be well over one million.

With one recent acquisition, the Forest Preserve District has already begun to look toward its future land needs. On April 4, 2000, the district purchased the 615-acre St. James Farm "with a life estate and conservation easement." This is not a farm in the ordinary sense, but rather a country estate in Warrenville. It belongs to the family of Brooks McCormick, former head of International Harvester, a firm founded by his great-uncle, Cyrus McCormick.

The property will not be available to the public immediately. The "life estate" provision will leave it in the possession of the family, but the white and oak woodlands on the property will stay intact for now and will serve the public in future generations. Until then, local residents will probably continue to view the estate much as the forest preserve's web site describes—as "shrouded in mystery" and "something out of Brigadoon."

What the district needs most is additional forest preserves like Fullersburg Woods. This charming area of trees surrounds a portion of Salt Creek. It has a nature center, paths with interpretative signage and Old Graue Mill, an historic structure with the milling machinery still in operating condition. Before the Civil War, the mill was a stop on the Underground Railroad.

Waterfall Glen is DuPage County's largest nature preserve. Surprisingly, the area is named not after its man-made waterfall, but for Seymour "Bud" Waterfall, an early DuPage County Forest Preserve president.

Lake County Forest Preserves

County population: 1990—516,418; 2000—644,356

For most of the twentieth century, Lake County had no forest preserves. Only in the late 1950s did it commit itself to developing a district. The county's shortsightedness was due in part to the fact that it is bordered on the east by Lake Michigan and is peppered with lakes, large and small, which already provided considerable recreational opportunities. The consequences can be seen in the forested areas lost to urban uses.

One of the most important sites in the more than 18,000 acres now preserved, protected and developed by the Forest District is the Lakewood Forest Preserve. This area also contains the county's historical museum.

In April 1999 the residents of Lake County approved a $55 million forest preserves bond issue. The money will be used to purchase additional green space, restore more habitats for rare native plants and animals, and increase nature trails. The goal of the Forest Preserve District is to protect 26,000 acres of forest land in all.

Within a year of the referendum, the county had added eight pieces of land, consisting of 751 acres, with several more to be added in the near future. Among the purchases were the 23-acre Lake Carina along with an adjacent wetland, savanna and prairie. Other acquired properties have included oak woodland, old farm fields, lakeshore, a wetland fen and an addition to the forest preserve's self-described "crown jewel—the Des Plaines River Greenway, a 7,500-acre ribbon of Forest Preserves.

In 2000 the district also received a state Open Space and Land Acquisition and Development grant of $400,000.

McHenry County Conservation District

County population: 1990—183,241; 2000—260,077

The McHenry County Conservation District is little more than 30 years old, the newest of this area's preservation districts. Its largest preserve is Glacial Park, south of Richmond on Illinois Route 31. Although the county uses the name "conservation district" instead of "forest preserve" as in neighboring counties, its mission of "preserving natural areas and open spaces for the educational and environmental benefits of present and future generations" is the same.

Among its recent acquisitions are:

1. A parcel of 45.75 acres directly across U.S. Highway 14 from the Woodstock Center.

2. An 87.15-acre site bordering the Bystricky Prairie, one of the last untouched black soil prairies in the state. The new acquisition supports a population of white lady's slipper orchids.

17. The CHICAGO Botanic Garden:
TEN SECRETS

Time and nature conspire here, with results that are at once astounding and serene.

—JAY PRIDMORE, *A GARDEN FOR ALL SEASONS*

Each year, close to a million people from around the world come to visit the Chicago Botanic Garden, a collection of 385 acres of land and lagoons in north suburban Glencoe. This special place, maintained by the Chicago Horticultural Society, consists of more than 20 serene and peaceful garden settings, including Japanese, dwarf conifer and English walled gardens.

Often, when a person experiences the Botanic Garden for the first time, he or she is surprised at the depth of its beauty. One has difficulty anticipating how dramatic, fascinating and charming the gardens truly are.

The gardens continue to amaze even its most frequent visitors, who might discover a previously unknown path leading into the rose garden, or a new spot on the lagoon where the view seems like the vision of a distant, exotic land.

The Chicago Botanic Garden is filled with secrets that defy expectations. Even the following pages of photographs and descriptions cannot prepare the reader for what awaits. Instead, this list of ten secrets simply

Some of the birds of the Chicago Botanic Garden (Chicago Botanic Garden/Linda Oyama Bryan)

points the way, providing the visitor with more opportunities to discover the unexpected.

These secrets include:

1. The Off-the-Map Suzanne S. Dixon Tallgrass Prairie

This tallgrass area is extraordinarily beautiful, especially in early fall. It is alive with birds, and colors beyond one's imagination. Yet many visitors go the Chicago Botanic Garden and see little of this prairie—or miss it altogether.

The simple fact is that many people tire before discovering it. It is the area farthest from the entrance and a long walk away from any other garden setting. In addition, the prairie is not on either the bike route or the "Bright

THE BEAUTY OF THE CHICAGO WILDERNESS

Encounters Tram Route," nor is it featured prominently on Botanic Garden maps. The popular railroad brochure map of the gardens indicates it only by means of an arrow. On the general map passed out to visitors, the site of the prairie is marked merely with a small dot and a number.

The prairie and lagoons (Chicago Botanic Garden/ William Biderbost)

Although these factors explain why the area is often overlooked, they should not be taken as excuses to ignore it. The prairie is as unique and beautiful as it is isolated. It is a treasure and ought not be a lost one.

2. The "Missing" McDonald Woods and Nature Trail

These make up another isolated but enriching area of the Chicago Botanic Garden. They are located east of the parking area, while most individuals will set off in the opposite direction, towards the Gateway Center that welcomes visitors.

The area consists of 110 acres of trees and trails. Considerable effort and research has gone into restoring the woods to its original habitat, which supports hickory, oak and other native trees as well as such woodland

Swans in the lagoons (Chicago Botanic Garden/ Joanne Dahlberg)

plants as trilliums. The staff worked to rid the woods of invasive plants such as the blackthorn. As a result, they were able to recapture native communities of both plants and animals.

3. The Unnoted Birds

According to its literature, one of the purposes of the Botanic Garden is to provide visiting and nesting birds with sources of food and water. The garden's staff has worked with great success to encourage the presence of many species, including the often hard-to-attract purple martin.

In a walk of less than an hour through the gardens, the author encountered a loon, egrets, ducks, swans, a hummingbird, warblers and goldfinches. An attentive birder would have seen many times more species. Still, few people realize the extent of the garden's bird population.

Unfortunately, there are no signs or literature to help visitors locate and identify the birds. In the future, hopefully, a booklet or at least a pamphlet will be issued, one that will help people appreciate the birds of the Chicago Botanic Garden.

4. The Unobserved Collections of Trees

Often, a visitor to the Chicago Botanic Garden is so enthralled by the splendor of the flowers, sculptures, lagoons and horticultural settings that he or she fails to notice the trees.

Trees adorn the Botanic Garden (Chicago Botanic Garden/William Biderbost)

Many of these, however, are just as deserving of special attention as the other plants. Some of the birches, for example, have been painstakingly imported from Siberia and other distant habitats around the world.

The gardens' managers might do well to find a way to highlight some of their trees—perhaps as the Morton Arboretum does, with its "Tree of the Month" program. It would be everyone's gain.

5. The Now-Reachable Spider Island

Spider Island has long been a small jewel of greenery, flowers and trees in the gardens' main lagoon. Until just recently, however, it remained unreachable to all except those gardeners responsible for developing and maintaining it.

THE CHICAGO BOTANIC GARDEN: TEN SECRETS

Now, a 110-foot handcrafted bridge of rough-hewn black locust connects it with the Main Island. A curving path leads through naturalist plantings of trees, herbaceous plants and grasses to a small seating area on the south side of the island.

6. The Latest Addition to the Bonsai Collection

In 2000, a bonsai master in Japan made a significant contribution of 20 rare bonsai plants. This addition has made the Chicago Botanic Garden's collection of these miniature plants one of the largest in the United States.

The newly acquired specimens could not be immediately be put on display because some have to go through a recovery stage and others are in quarantine. At this point, their introduction remains a surprise waiting to happen.

7. The Greenhouses

Ah, to see an orchid bloom in mid-February!

Here, in houses made of glass, a visitor can walk through a dry desert or visit tropical plants even as the snow might be falling outside. These are places into which a stroller or runner can step and breathe warmer air, or where an amateur gardener can find inspiration and new ideas on what to plant in the spring.

The Botanic Garden contains three different greenhouses:

- The dry desert greenhouse offers more than cacti and plants from the American Southwest; it provides a visitor with an opportunity to experience plants from other deserts in countries throughout the world. One such plant is the cow's horn from South Africa.

- The tropical flower greenhouse is where a visitor finds St. John's bread. This plant, which produces carob flour used for baking bread, can also provide feed for cattle and serve as a coffee substitute during times of shortage, as there was during World War II.

- The third greenhouse, which specializes in plants that can be adapted for home use, displays everything from inexpensive bromeliads to *topiaries*, trees and shrubs which have been pruned into living sculptures. Two of the sculptures here are in the shape of a horse and a dog. An interpretative sign explains that the Romans developed the art of topiary in 4 BC.

8. The Unheralded Flower Collections

All over the Chicago Botanic Garden, groups of flowers flourish that are not directly connected with any of the distinct garden areas. The flowers are not grouped by type, but are scattered together throughout the grounds. Nevertheless, the planters and gardeners see each type of flower as a separate collection. Thus, the grounds can claim a not only a substantial viburnum collection but also the largest daffodil collection anywhere in the Midwest.

9. Evening Island's Newly Added New American Garden

Prior to the recent addition of this garden, Evening Island, located south of Main Island, was noted principally for the landmark carillon there.

Work on the new five-acre garden began in the spring of 2000 and represented one of the largest single garden developments ever undertaken at the Chicago Botanic Garden. The natural, seemingly "undeveloped" design of the area is characteristic of the New American Garden style created by Wolfgang Oehme and James van Sweden. It utilizes prairie plants and grasses. Distinct garden areas will include a hillside garden, a knoll garden, an evergreen grove and woodland gardens.

The New American Garden provides a model for people who want to use such a naturalistic look to transform their lawns, yards and side lots. It will also offer seasonal changes with the plantings of spring bulbs, summer perennials, fall foliage and colorful willow and dogwood branches in winter.

10. The Fact That on Certain Days, Visitors Can Watch Sunrises and Sunsets

The Chicago Botanic Garden is open daily from 8 a.m. to sunset. These hours offer the visitor the opportunity to view the gardens at many different time of day, in vastly different lights.

The gardens are open every day of the year except Christmas.

18. The MORTON Arboretum:
TREES TO WHICH WE CAN RELATE

Plant trees.

—MORTON FAMILY MOTTO

The Morton Arboretum in suburban Lisle has more than 3,300 kinds of trees, shrubs and other plants on 1,700 acres of woodlands, wetlands, restored native prairie and gardens.

The value of this DuPage County land on the open market would be staggering. To the people who make use of this extraordinary arboretum, it is incalculable.

The future, ours and our neighbors', is here.

"A man does not plant a tree for himself," Alexander Smith wrote. "He plants it for posterity."

This is what the Morton Arboretum's founder Joy Morton understood. He and his successors brought trees here from around the world, studied them for generations and tested to determine whether they could survive and prosper in northern Illinois.

Some eighty rings have been added to the older trees here since Morton bequeathed the land in 1922.

Fittingly, a tree stands sentinel over the sign welcoming people to the Morton Arboretum (Morton Arboretum)

A new enthusiasm regarding the natural beauty of the Chicago area has given nature centers such as the Morton Arboretum a more immediate sense of purpose. They now have the advantage of meeting a clearly perceived need.

Over the years, those who have worked or volunteered at the Arboretum, the Chicago Botanic Garden, the Ladd Arboretum, Fullersburg Woods, the Little Red School House and many other local nature centers have helped spark this interest and appreciation. Their work with trees, shrubs and flowers can be seen today on the streets of the city and suburbs.

WHERE THE BEAUTIFICATION BEGINS

Many of the species of trees beautifying Chicago's streets and parks were studied and appreciated at the Morton Arboretum first. Arboretum arborists, naturalists, gardeners and landscapers planted and evaluated the trees to see how they would do under urban conditions such as salt and poor soil.

The Morton Arboretum, however, inspires more than learning. Many visitors take no lessons, practice no landscaping and study nothing about gardening. Yet, they revel in pretty flowers, brightly colored leaves and a dramatically restored prairie.

Visitors examine leaves and twigs (Morton Arboretum)

The Arboretum displays many trees in groups of 20 to 40 and offers hills of spruces, pines and hemlocks. Twelve miles of one-way, winding roads help visitors view or stop off at the various tree collections, lakes, woods, gardens and fields. The 25 miles of trails allow people to get up close and experience nature in its many habitats.

TEN TREES TO GET TO KNOW AT THE MORTON ARBORETUM

The Morton Arboretum is ultimately about trees. The following is a list that can help the visitor better appreciate them individually. Much of the following material is based on "Tree of the Month" write-ups compiled by the Arboretum staff:

1. The White Oak

*The Illinois Millennium Landmark Tree is a white oak located
at the Arboretum.*

The white oak is the Illinois State tree and the Arboretum has many of
them. In the year 2000, one particular specimen was chosen to be the "Illinois Millennium Landmark Tree."

The America the Beautiful Fund, part of the White House Millennium
Council's Green Initiative, selected a stately tree on the Arboretum's west
side for the honor. It is just north of Lake Marmo, a hundred yards east of
the roadway. A plaque recognizing the tree was erected in a ceremony on
July 9, 2000.

The Millennium Landmark Tree, approximately 250 years old, predates
both Illinois' statehood and the American Revolution.

White oaks are tall, often 80 feet high. The word "white" in the tree's name
comes from its gray, scaly bark, lighter than that of most oaks. Its leaves
are dark green, and turn a rich, handsome reddish brown in autumn.

Specimens of white oaks can be found throughout the Arboretum; a group of them grow in Sargeant Glade near parking lot 20.

Nature writer Donald Culross Peattie described the white oak as "a second home, an outdoor mansion of shade and greenery and leafy music."

2. Dawn-Redwood

Once thought extinct. For years, naturalists were familiar only with fossils of it.

In *The Living Tree,* H. L. Edlin wrote of the Dawn-Redwood:

[It] created a sensation in botanical circles when it was first discovered as a living tree . . . previously it had only been known as a fossil and it seemed as though the dead had come to life.

The Dawn-Redwood tree was grown with seeds from trees found growing along streams in remote valleys of China. Though it bears its seeds in cones like an evergreen, it does not retain its leaves year-round.

This tree is located along the Thornhill Trail.

3. Katsura Tree

Arguably the most beautiful or at least the most appreciated tree at the Arboretum.

This particularly fine specimen, a large and full tree, stands opposite the main entrance of the Arboretum's Research and Administration Center, showcasing its flowers, leaves and character.

Arboretum literature on the katsura tree quotes Michael A. Dirr:

One of my favorite trees, overwhelming in over-all attractiveness.
If I could use only one tree, this would be my first [choice].

The katsura is native to the cool, temperate forest of Japan. It is a popular tree used in the landscaping of residences, commercial buildings, parks and golf courses.

THE MORTON ARBORETUM: TREES TO WHICH WE CAN RELATE

4. Sugar Maple

October brings out spectacular leaf colors: brilliant yellow, burnt orange and touches of red.

As its name indicates, this tree produces sugar. Tapped in the late winter, a mature tree can yield 30 gallons of sap. Boiled down, these would produce a gallon of syrup or four pounds of sugar.

The sugar maple has a sensitive root system that needs room to grow and does not tolerate salt.

This is a beautiful tree even before its green leaves transition to their fall colors.

The Morton Arboretum's *Visitor Map and Guide* lists two areas of maple trees on the park's east side.

5. Bur Oak

Bold, craggy and majestic.

This tree stands out and spreads out wherever it grows. A remarkable specimen can be found near parking lot 18 and is visible from well up the road.

A bur (or burr) is defined as "the rough or prickly envelope that contains a fruit." In this case, it is the heavily fringed acorn cup.

The bur oak was a key component of the oak savannas that often adjoined tallgrass prairies throughout the Midwest a hundred years ago.

6. Flowering Dogwood

This author's favorite.

When the compiler of this book was a young boy, he discovered a flowering dogwood in the center of a nearby woods and returned to visit it often. He has found it impossible to draw up a list of ten trees that did not include this species.

Its flowers are singularly beautiful in mid-May, but this tree also has striking leaves in summer and fascinating colors in fall.

Both Native Americans and pioneers used the bark to help fight fevers, chills and malaria.

Among the many sites in the Arboretum where flowering dogwoods can be found are on Hemlock Hill, south of Lake Marmo, and along Ridge Road off the Geographic Trail.

7. Shagbark Hickory

> *President Andrew Jackson was known as "Old Hickory" for being as rugged as the wood of this tree.*

This was the American pioneers' favorite tree. It provided them with lumber, fuel and edible nuts, and became scarce in the nation's forests as a result of its popularity.

Its green wood is burned to cure smoked meats and its lumber used for hardwood furniture. A cord of its slow-burning firewood is almost equal in thermal power to a ton of anthracite coal.

An exceptional specimen of this tree is found on the west edge of parking lot 25.

8. Gingko or Maidenhair Tree

> *While awkward and angular when young, it becomes beautifully sculpted as it matures. As such, it has been described as "spiritual."*

Joy Morton loved the ginkgoes; hence, they are planted throughout the Arboretum. A grove of them greets cars on the north side of the road as they start to drive through the east side of the park. They were planted in 1926, apparently with Morton's personal help.

The gingko is a low-branched, ornamental tree that invites people to climb up in it. The fan-shaped leaves are a fresh green. In fall they turn a bright yellow, drop from the tree and carpet the ground.

The gingko, which is from China, is ancient, as shown by fossil records. It has no living relatives.

The Arboretum suggests that any-one looking for a specific species or specimen of a tree is welcome to drop in at the Visitors Center for help or directions.

9. Eastern White Pine

In the early days of the United States it was said a squirrel could travel its entire life in a straight line across the North-east, going all the way on white pines.

This pine is a tall, fast-growing tree that can reach 150 feet in height. It is also a spreading tree known for its long, shining needles and pendant cones.

Under ordinary circumstances, it grows and transplants well, and is often found in groves and forests. However, the white pine is highly susceptible to almost all maladies with which our society confronts it, including salt, air pollution and deforestation.

Pinewood is soft and workable. It has been used for everything from ship masts to matchsticks, from coffins to inexpensive furniture.

One particularly interesting specimen of white pine is in the Arbore-tum's Eastern U.S. Wetlands collection located on the north side of the Main Route.

10. Accolade Elm

Remarkably immune to the Dutch elm disease.

The parents of this 78-year-old tree were a Japanese elm and a Wilson elm in Boston's Arnold Arboretum. It came to The Morton Arboretum as a seed in 1924.

It is considered salt-tolerant and unusually free of disease.

The Morton Arboretum is home to the nation's largest collection of elm species and Arboretum researchers are leaders in the effort to breed elm trees resistant to Dutch elm disease, the scourge of the American elms that once lined many shady city streets.

The accolade elm's leaves are glossier and an even deeper green than those of the American elm. Their fall color is a bright yellow.

One specimen of the tree is found south of the Founder's Room, Thorn-hill Conference Center.

*A winter scene
(Morton
Arboretum)*

19. The Peggy NOTEBAERT Nature Museum:
A BUTTERFLY HAVEN AND
NATURAL SCIENCE ACADEMY

Chicago is a wild place, not by virtue of its nightlife or crime, but because it shelters pristine landscapes, untamed plants and animals, and secluded retreats where greenery reigns.

—ISABEL S. ABRAMS, *THE NATURE OF CHICAGO*

The Peggy Notebaert Nature Museum, on the shore of the North Pond in Chicago's Lincoln Park, is a showcase of living nature—tallgrass prairies, trees, flowers, beavers and butterflies.

What a contrast this new museum is to many of the nature museums of the past, which were filled only with well-worn illustrations, stuffed animals, dusty exhibits and dead leaves!

Even more importantly, the focus has changed. Older museums concentrated on collections, research and a formal attempt to educate people about nature. Today, according to the new museum's brochure, the focus is on "exploring and nurturing our relationship with the environment."

Located at 2430 North Cannon Drive, the new Peggy Notebaert Nature Museum is the creation of the Chicago Academy of Sciences, and represents a true departure for the 142-year-old organization, which also runs an older, more conventional museum on North Clark Street.

YOU TOO CAN HAVE BUTTERFLIES

(The following is from a Peggy Notebaert Nature Museum pamphlet:)

The more hours of sunlight in your garden, the longer your butterflies will stay warm enough to find food, mates and egg-laying sites. The sun's warmth also helps eggs develop more quickly. In the sun, your flowers will bloom sooner and produce more food for caterpillars and adult butterflies. Some shade is important to provide a cool place for resting from the heat. Also, wind can affect butterfly behavior, therefore some protection is necessary with fences, trees, or bushes.

A carefully selected mix of annuals and perennials will ensure that there will always be plants blooming to provide a continuous source of nectar for butterflies. The annuals will bloom all summer, and the perennials will grow back every year. The site can be any size; in a window box, a raised bed, a perennial border, or a large expanse of prairie. However, avoid using pesticides as chemicals that kill pests will kill butterflies too.

The Notebaert Museum was completed in 1999 on land made available by the Chicago Park District. The building, pleasing to the eye, was designed by architect Ralph Johnson of Perkins & Will.

The structure is delightfully open to the sky and the natural environment around it. It is also an example of user-friendly architecture in the best tradition of Chicago design. The ultra-modern building offers spacious windows, computer stations, imaginative play exhibits, outdoor trails and live butterflies.

It attempts to tell the story not of far-away places or times, but of Chicago's own ecosystems and habitats.

The museum's best-loved attraction by far is the Judy Istock Butterfly Haven on the second floor. It is a high-ceilinged room full of flowering and aromatic plants, and, most special of all, fluttering, distinctly colored butterflies.

Here, a multitude of them dart about the room, landing on plants, people—any surface they can find. Even if a visitor knows what to expect, he or she reacts with surprised amazement upon experiencing this butterfly sanctuary firsthand.

The staff is currently breeding five different species of butterflies to populate this haven. They include cabbage whites, orange sulphurs, buckeyes, painted ladies and black swallowtails.

The museum does more than let people experience butterflies. It also tells their story. Particularly significant for Chicagoans is the story of the monarch, which visits the area on its migration to and from its breeding grounds in Mexico.

The monarchs fly 2,500 miles from Chicago to Mexico. They cover 20 to 50 miles a day, and the entire trip lasts approximately 125 days. They journey together and so many can land in a single pine tree that its branches sometimes break. They put mating on hold until their voyage to Mexico is completed. The return to the Chicago area by the monarchs, on the other hand, may take two or three generations to complete.

SUGGESTED PLANTS TO INCLUDE AS NECTAR SOURCES:

Alum root	*Great lobelia*
Bee balm	*Ironweed*
Bergamot	*Joe Pye weed*
Black-eyed susan	*Milkweed*
Blazing star	*New England aster*
Blue verain	*Purple coneflower*
Boneset	*Rattlesnake master*
Butterfly weed	*Thistle*
Cardinal flower	*Wild quinine*
Dogbane	

This museum's interpretative portrayal of prairies, savannas, dunes and ponds in the Chicago area is well suited for children, even those of a young age. They can walk through the simulated underground of a tallgrass prairie with long, cloth hangings to represent its deep roots. Another exhibit allows them to crawl into a snug room built like a beaver lodge. Before they go through it, they can don outfits that make them look and feel like the wood-gnawing animals.

Youngsters can also use a room full of computers to engage in an interactive encounter with aspects of environmental science.

The tallgrass prairie, savanna and dunes exhibits, while less hands-on than the computer room, present engaging information about what makes these habitats unique.

At this point, the museum still has room for extensive additional displays. This area might be used effectively in partnership with the various other organizations that make up the Chicago Wilderness.

20. Some CHICAGO AREA
Naure Interpretive Centers:
WHERE THE INTRODUCTIONS
BEGIN

I went to the woods because I wished to live deliberately, to front only the essential facts of life, and see if I could not learn what it had to teach, and not, when I came to die, discover that I had not lived.

—HENRY DAVID THOREAU

Nature, like beauty, can neither be argued nor taught. At best, it can be presented, introduced, as one person might be to another. The nature interpretative centers of the Chicago area afford this opportunity for introductions.

Here are some of them:

1. North Park Village Nature Center

5801 North Pulaski Road, Chicago.

Located on the Northwest Side of the city, this nature center includes trails through woodland, wetland and savanna, with volunteers to help interpret what the visitor sees. No bikes. No smoking. No skiing.

2. River Trail Nature Center

3120 North Milwaukee Avenue, Northbrook.

One of the most exciting places to experience the Des Plaines River. The early Native American residents of the area are celebrated here, as is

Chicago's "first permanent resident," pioneer Jean Baptiste Point DuSable. Best time to visit: for the Fall Harvest and Honey Festival.

3. Crabtree Nature Center

Palatine Road, west of Stover Road, Barrington.

A superb spot for getting acquainted with birds, either by using the not-for-hunting duck blind on Crabtree Lake or attending the center's Migratory Bird Day events. Also, the grounds offer an interesting, particularly challenging prairie walk.

4. Sand Ridge Nature Center

15890 Paxton Avenue, South Holland.

The sand ridges and low swales were created thousands of years ago when Lake Chicago began to shrink down to become Lake Michigan. Its 5.7

THE BEAUTY OF THE CHICAGO WILDERNESS

miles of trails lead through woodlands, ridges and wetlands. Special programs center around the log cabins that constitute part of the center.

5. Ladd Arboretum and Ecology Center

2024 McCormick Boulevard, southwest of
Green Bay Road, Evanston.

The staff of the Ecology Center located on the grounds of the arboretum have a strong reputation as friendly and helpful. The Arboretum's International Peace Garden includes native trees from more than 120 countries as well as the Woman's Terrace along the banks of the North Channel.

6. Heller Nature Center

2821 Ridge Road, Highland Park.

This site is covered mainly by deciduous, oak-dominated woodland. The small pond has an aeration system powered with solar energy. Ask about the center's midwinter owling program.

7. Fullersburg Woods

On Spring Road north of Ogden Avenue and
west of York Road in Hinsdale.

The Environmental Education Center in Fullersburg Woods introduced to the area the idea of renting headsets for a 1.3-mile interpretative nature walk. The 221-acre nature preserve has five miles of trails and is connected to Graue Mill, the only operating waterwheel gristmill in the state.

8. Little Red School House Nature Center

9800 South Willow Springs Road, Willow Springs.

The center, at the heart of the incredible natural treasures of the Palos area, is the starting point for hikes to the Long John Slough and surrounding woodlands. The programs of its interpretative center are especially kid-friendly.

9. Thatcher Woods and Hal Tyrrell Trailside Museum

738 Thatcher Avenue, River Forest.

The museum provides guides who take visitors through the woodlands, wetlands and prairie. The area was a favorite of Native Americans and the nature center programs focus on their historic presence in the area. People can bring wounded animals here to receive medical attention, as this is the home of the county's Wildlife Rehabilitation Center.

10. Edward L. Ryerson Conservation Area

Northwest of Deerfield off Riverwoods Road.

The area along the Des Plaines is noted for its wildflowers, virgin forest and animal life. It includes 6.5 miles of interconnecting trails. In the winter, the staff of the education center offers programs on such topics as animal tracking, skiing and the use of a compass.

CHICAGO *Treasures*

21. The Most Beautiful

Architectural Sites of CHICAGO:

A SUBJECTIVE LIST

Chicago takes pride in building things in a big, substantial, broad way.

—FRANK LLOYD WRIGHT, *LONDON LECTURES,* 1939

1. The Rookery Building

209 South LaSalle Street.

This building always charms me, affects me like a strain of music which fortunately combines delicacy with strength.

—HARRIET MONROE, FOUNDER OF *POETRY: A MAGAZINE OF VERSE*

The Rookery Building, on the southeast corner of LaSalle and Adams, is beautiful, but in an intimate rather than an awe-demanding way. This unassuming quality is the essence of most great architecture, especially in Chicago.

The Rookery Building, solid and sturdy, has been called "self-confident." It hides delightful secrets and is the work of two of the most innovative architects in American history: John Wellborn Root and Frank Lloyd Wright.

Inside the building, secrets can be found. The first is a stunning atrium and light court that features a staircase, metalwork, lighting and ornamentation created by Frank Lloyd Wright. The second, poetic and captivating, is a stairwell that spirals upwards from the mezzanine.

JOHN WELLBORN ROOT

The Rookery, designed by the firm of Burnham and Root, was completed in 1888. Root, at this point in his short career, was a master of ornamentation and it shows up in the intricate design of the facade and entranceway. All this decoration is attractive and inviting, but John Wellborn Root kept everything subordinate to the form of this building, which is eloquent, self-assured and perfectly proportioned.

On three occasions over the past 25 years, the building, atrium and stair-well have all been wonderfully refurbished, renovated or restored.

Robie House (Richard Nickel/ Commission on Chicago Landmarks)

The Rookery, a world-reknown treasure, is a sentimental favorite of the *aficionado* of exquisite or exciting architecture.

2. Frederick C. Robie House

5757 South Woodlawn Avenue.

> *Of the more than 75 buildings that Frank Lloyd Wright designed for the Chicago area, none is more famous or has been more influential than the Robie House.*
>
> —THE COMMISSION ON CHICAGO HISTORICAL AND ARCHITECTURAL LANDMARKS

Located in the Hyde Park neighborhood, the Frederick C. Robie House was Frank Lloyd Wright's best residential design. We have his own word upon it, given in 1959 when he revisited Robie House just before his death.

This is where Wright perfected his Prairie Style residential architecture. The house's sweeping, horizontal design broke sharply with the two- and

A SPACEWRIGHT

The Robie House, built in 1909 for the family of a bicycle manufacturer, showed how people could live in a horizontal space more interestingly and freely than in a conventional multi-level structure. It was a dramatic discovery.

three-story designs of the past. Its geometrical lines come together in a usefulness and beauty that validates this as a house, a home, for its time and the future.

In the 1993 edition of *Chicago's Famous Buildings,* Franz Schulze and Kevin Harrington write of Robie House:

> Adapted to a narrow city lot, it nonetheless achieves an amplitude of form enlivened by a powerful, tightly organized interpenetration of masses. The long limestone sills, the broad overhanging roofs, even the slender "Roman bricks," contribute to the horizontality said by Wright to reflect the Midwestern prairie—hence the name standardly applied to the style. Interior space flows freely between living and dining room around the great hearth.

3. Carson Pirie Scott & Co. Building (Formerly Schlesinger and Mayer Co.)

One South State Street.

As Chicagoans of 1900 stepped within the doors of Sullivan's great Schlesinger and Mayer department store . . . the noise and ugliness of the street were transformed into quiet serenity and elegance.

—Hugh Dalziel Duncan, *Culture and Democracy*

The Carson Pirie Scott & Co. Building on the southeast corner of State and Madison is as clearly a work of art as any commercial building in Chicago. The store was designed by Louis Sullivan in 1899, with an addition by him in 1903–4, and another by D. H. Burnham and Company in 1906. Burnham followed Sullivan's style, altering only the top floor. This department store created a basic design for retail stores that has been used ever since, and answered the fundamental question, "How can an architect help a merchant attract, please and serve customers?"

CARSON'S: THE RIGHT BUILDING IN THE RIGHT PLACE

The elaborate ornamental latticework that frames the main door of Carson's provides a glimpse of nature and a moment of reflection at State and Madison, long called the busiest corner in America.

By featuring ornamentation that reflects nature, framing products in windows on the street level and making use of generous natural lighting, this department store design can display merchandise better than any more elaborate means.

The interior of the building offers a simple but revolutionary design, a grid of space much like a warehouse, interrupted only by columns housing the steel internal supports of the building.

In many ways, the grandest, most beautiful aspect of the State Street store is still the "Chicago windows," so called because the design originated in this city. If we look at other century-old commercial buildings, the benefits of these windows become clear: instead of the traditional

THE MOST BEAUTIFUL ARCHITECTURAL SITES OF CHICAGO: A SUBJECTIVE LIST

double-hung window, which was meant to shut off light, this design used a large center pane with narrower panes on each side to invite light in.

This building was groundbreaking and functional, and exactly what Sullivan intended: a beautiful way to package merchandise on a grand scale.

4. The Reliance Building

32 North State Street.

The Reliance is without question one of the 19th Century's most artistic achievements. It is daring in design and construction technique, while solving completely utilitarian demands.

—THE COMMISSION ON CHICAGO HISTORICAL AND ARCHITECTURAL LANDMARKS

Recent renovation breathed life and excitement back into this 1895 jewel. The restaurant on the first floor is called the Atwood Café for its architect, Charles Atwood. The inn which the building now houses is named the Hotel Burnham, after Daniel Burnham, whose architectural firm designed the structure.

The building was started in 1890 by John Wellborn Root, and finished in 1895 after the World's Columbian Exposition. Root had died in the meantime and Atwood, an architect who had served under Burnham at the fair, completed it.

The beautiful, open appearance of the building was achieved through the use of Chicago windows.

Charles Atwood was a New York architect in fact and tradition. But when he followed Root's lead and finished the design of the Reliance, he created what the Commission on Chicago Historical and Architectural Landmarks called "a triumph of the structure and principles of Chicago school

A COMPLETELY NEW LOOK IN ARCHITECTURE

Through a dramatic new use of windows, the Reliance Building contributed a new sense of openness to modern architectural design. For the first time a building's windows, rather than its bricks, seemed to be its skin.

The Monadnock's internal design is equally stunning. Its ironwork and elevator designs are especially striking. The lobby provides one of the best surviving examples of an original Tiffany mosaic.

design," adding that its "grace, transparency and exquisite proportions transcend commercial necessity to become fine art."

The first commercial tenant of the building was Carson Pirie & Company, which later added the name of Scott and moved into its present location at State and Madison.

5. The Monadnock Block

53 West Jackson Boulevard.

An amazing cliff of brickwork, rising sheer and stark, with a subtlety of line and surface, a direct singleness of purpose, that gave one the thrill of romance.

—ARCHITECT LOUIS SULLIVAN

Sullivan's comparison of the John Wellborn Root's Monadnock with a sheer and stark cliff is indeed appropriate. This building would be at home as easily in a mountain range as on the south side of Chicago's Loop. In fact, the building was named after a mountain in New England.

Its limits are many. It is awkwardly thin (because it sits on a half-block). The structure has next to no ornamentation on its exterior (because the clients, Peter Brooks and Owen Aldis, did not want it). And the north half demonstrates wall-bearing construction, which required the street-level walls to be six-foot–thick blocks of stone.

No other commercial venture, however, quite tells the story of the great discoveries of the Chicago School of Architecture as dramatically as the Monadnock, which is two separate slab-thin buildings. The pair fit tightly on a city block surrounded by Jackson, Plymouth Court, Van Buren and

Dearborn. Plymouth Court, by cutting through what would be a full city block, actually turns this into a long, narrow half-block.

The double structure has four sections, each with its own entrance. Each of these portions is named for a New England mountain.

The north half of the Monadnock, constructed in 1891 by Burnham and Root, is the tallest outside wall–bearing commercial structure ever built— 16 stories or 197 feet high.

Despite its awkwardness, this building that dates to the years of architectural transformation is extraordinarily beautiful. The clients' request for little or no ornamentation challenged the young architectural genius John Wellborn Root to forgo all distractions and make the Monadnock simpler than any large building of the past.

Root seized the moment and changed the course of architecture by showing that form and proportion are actually freed up when unnecessary ornamentation is dispensed with. The structure is indeed a cliff, a mountain that rises elegantly on the south side of the Loop.

The south half of the Monadnock was completed in 1893 by the architectural firm of Holabird and Roche. By then, Root had died and Daniel Burnham was the head architect for the World's Columbian Exposition.

This building, face-to-face with the north half, tells a different part of the story of Chicago commercial architecture in that period. Instead of load-bearing walls, the new firm used steel-skeletal construction. This method was developed in Chicago in 1885 for William Le Baron Jenny's Home Insurance Building, the world's first skyscraper.

What is ultimately amazing is that the two parts of the Monadnock seem to belong to one another, a relationship that has lasted for more than 100 years.

6. The 333 North Wacker Drive Building

This 36-floor granite and glass building is one of the finest additions to Chicago's downtown area.

—Ira Bach and Susan Wolfson, *Chicago on Foot*

The 333 North Wacker Drive Building is a structure which the casual passerby and professional architect alike admire. Set on a triangular lot at the bend in the Chicago River, the building features a stunning 365-foot curved, green glass façade.

The windows reflect not only the water but also the panorama across the river from them, including the trees, the Merchandise Mart and the Apparel Center. The enormous Mart is now best viewed across the river in reflected glory.

Chicagoans will tell you that at certain times of the morning, the effect is magical, giving a distinct impressionist image of the building's neighbors.

Architects call this first Chicago design by the New York firm of Kohn Pedersen Fox "postmodern."

It offers retail space at street level and offices above.

7. The John Hancock Center

875 North Michigan Avenue.

By far the finest and most interesting of Chicago's giant buildings, the assertive, muscular John Hancock Center claims our attention as powerfully as the tapering masonry Monadnock.

—Franz Schulze and Kevin Harrington, *Chicago's Famous Buildings*

The John Hancock, from its very beginning, has been special to Chicagoans.

Each day in the late 1960s, as the Hancock climbed closer to its full height of 100 stories, Chicago residents grew more surprised and amazed. As the structure lost its awkwardness and slowly began to soar, they wondered that their city would soon be home to the tallest building in the world.

They also marveled at the black aluminum braces that created 18-story–high Xs, and were amazed to learn that they would not be hidden beneath cement or slabs of stone.

Finally, the TV towers on top brought this Skidmore, Owings & Merrill creation to its record-breaking height of 1,127 feet tall. For the first time, one piece of good old flat Chicago was visible from almost all over the city!

In the years to come, Chicago would build skyscrapers that rose even higher, but as the first Chicago building to be named the world's tallest in generations, the John Hancock retains its special place in the hearts of Chicagoans—just as the Empire State Building does for New Yorkers.

The John Hancock Center was designed in the great tradition of Chicago skyscrapers. This multi-use building demonstrates the proportionate directness of John Wellborn Root, the functionalism of Louis Sullivan and the "less is more" look of Mies van der Rohe.

It is an honest, innovative and basically simple building, the beauty of which grows on and surprises each viewer.

8. The Getty Tomb

The Getty Tomb (Commission on Chicago Landmarks)

Graceland Cemetery, 4001 North Clark Street

After leaving Graceland, you will undoubtedly agree that the Getty Tomb transcends in beauty all other monuments there.

—IRA BACH AND SUSAN WOLFSON, *CHICAGO ON FOOT*

Frank Lloyd Wright called the Getty Tomb in Graceland Cemetery on the city's North Side, "A great poem addressed to human sensibilities as such. Outside the realm of music what finer requiem?"

This work by Louis Sullivan stands alone and is obviously different from all other tombs and sculptures in the cemetery.

It is ornate and yet understated. The tomb's quiet, traditional shape affirms that this is a place where bodies are entombed. It seems to make a human statement about eternity by imprinting images of life on a building that denotes death, uniting these elements and leaving no loose ends.

THE MOST BEAUTIFUL ARCHITECTURAL SITES OF CHICAGO: A SUBJECTIVE LIST

Standing before it, one feels a message coming from it, an exquisite and significant one that speaks of life and death, happiness and sadness.

Not far away is Louis Sullivan's simple grave marker.

Sullivan crafted two other tombs, one for the Ryersons that is also in Graceland and another for the Wainwright family, which is in a St. Louis cemetery.

All three tell us that a human being has left his mark on life.

9. Evanston Public Library

Church Street and Orrington Avenue

It's more than a comfortable warehouse for our entire collection; it's actually a beautiful building.

—EVANSTON LIBRARY DIRECTOR NEAL NEY

Great architecture does not stand at a distance. It does not try to bedazzle like a fireworks display. A well-designed building—be it a house, barn or store—is, according to the dictum of Louis Sullivan, functional.

Inside the Evanston Public Library (Evanston Public Library)

THE MOST BEAUTIFUL ARCHITECTURAL SITES OF CHICAGO: A SUBJECTIVE LIST

The function of a public library is not simply to hold books, but also to invite people in to read and appreciate them. It is tragic for a library to be a grandiose classical bastion that seems designed only for the few, the sophisticated and the elite.

Yet such was the style in which America's libraries (and other public buildings) were constructed for more than a century. They were meant to overawe rather than beckon the public. The libraries attracted primarily the select, and so their policies focused on the elite as well. Louis Sullivan believed that people working in such classically-designed buildings ought to wear togas.

Evanston's current library, completed in 1994, replaced one that was a pseudo replica of a Greek temple. The design of the new building is Midwest Prairie School, and shows a healthy influence by the works of Louis Sullivan and, even more, his disciple Frank Lloyd Wright.

Where the old structure intimidated, the new one is warm and inviting.

10. The Water Tower and Pumping Station

806 and 811 North Michigan Avenue

A castellated monstrosity with pepperboxes stuck all over it.

—OSCAR WILDE

Chicago's Water Tower and its matching water pumping station across North Michigan Avenue neither represent nor inspire good architecture. A visitor finds them extraordinarily out of place in a city noted for straightforward, form-follows-function building construction.

These two structures, however, have been around since 1867 and have earned the city's appreciation as a tenacious old dog might—by surviving far longer than anyone had a right to expect.

Therein lies their beauty.

More than one and a third centuries after being built, the Water Tower now finds itself at the center of the city's posh commercial area. If buildings can be fortunate, then the Water Tower is indeed a lucky one. Not only was it the only public building to come out of the Chicago Fire still standing, but over the years it has also exchanged its boarding-house neighbors for a row of exclusive stores and hotels.

Its architect, William W. Boyington, designed the Water Tower and Pumping Station to camouflage the 138-foot standpipe used to even out the fluctuations in water pressure from Old Dally, the water pump for the North Side. To create the disguise, he used yellow dolomite quarried near Joliet and assembled it in a castellated Gothic architectural style.

Boyington's design, according to *Chicago's Famous Buildings,* was "an imitation of Gothic architecture so naïve that it seems original at points."

A CASTLE AGAINST ATTACKERS

"Castellated" refers to the use of battlements, in the style of those from which medieval bowmen could shoot their arrows to defend a castle against attackers. There is real reason to question the style's appropriateness for Chicago's Water Tower.

Chicagoans, nevertheless, remain proud of their Water Tower. They keep trying to spruce it up. In 2000, for example, the city redesigned the adjacent park, using plans formulated by Chicago's internationally acclaimed fashion photographer, Victor Skrebneski.

22. Built in the 1990s:

ENHANCEMENTS OF THE LOOP
AND RIVER NORTH AREAS

Of few modern cities can it be said, as of Chicago that in its architecture lies the history of the struggle for the form of a new civilization, the civilization of America.

—HUGH DALZIEL DUNCAN, *CULTURE AND DEMOCRACY*

During the 1990s, Chicago underwent an unusually active period of construction in the Loop and North River area. It was a period during which the city added many commercial and residential buildings to its skyline.

It was also a period of architectural transition, an eclectic era of postmodernism in which the past was inventively revisited and completely new ideas were explored.

Since then, the construction boom has continued. But the decade now over made a distinctive and innovative mark on architecture just short of the Chicago architectural revolution of a century before.

As the reader starts to examine the news buildings of the 1990s, he or she will begin to note some of the patterns that emerge:

- Chicago, architecturally, is not static, but continues to change.

- The city remains hungry to add commercial space.

- Many of the new buildings stand tall, wide and deep. In other words, they are massive.

- Two areas are especially favored: in or around the Loop and on the north side of the river.

- The buildings' architectural styles vary, as do the home bases and backgrounds of the architects who designed them.

- The buildings of the 1990s generally fit in well with the architecture of the city's past, much of which is more than 100 years old.

- Each structure represents an investment in the city's future as well as the conviction that Chicago will continue to grow and prosper.

- This new architecture has made the city much more fascinating and beautiful than before.

The following buildings were completed in the downtown area of Chicago in the 1990s:

1 North Franklin
Skidmore, Owings & Merrill, 1992

This structure, like several of Chicago's 1990s buildings, reflects the *Art Deco* style of the late 1920s and early 1930s. It was designed by Joseph Gonzalez, a partner in Skidmore. The 38-story structure has skin of pale granite, and it is topped with twin lighted towers that might be imagined as artistic beacons for airplanes or dirigibles.

311 South Wacker Drive Tower
Kohn Pederson Fox with *Harwood K. Smith and Partners, 1990*

What a contrast this structure presents to the Sears Tower just to the north! This building is the tallest reinforced concrete structure in the world, 65 stories or 970 feet. But its neighbor is 110 stories and 1,454 feet. While the tubular Sears is considered eloquently simple, the octagonal 311 South Wacker Drive structure is lit up like a Christmas tree by 2000 fluorescent bulbs. Atop it is a 70-foot cyclindric "water tower" that adds to its reputation as a most unusual building.

350 North LaSalle
Loebl, Schlossman & Hackl, 1990

This 15-story law office building, built of reinforced concrete, is across the street from the former traffic court building. It is on a sloping site north of the river and its unique feature is its red brick façade with window bays of green glass.

401 East Ontario
Nagle/Hartray & Associates, 1990

Captain Streeter, an early twentieth century Chicago boat captain and renegade, once laid claim to the land on which this apartment building was later built, and the area for blocks around. He would probably have used some choice phrases to describe the idea of constructing a 50-story skyscraper on his claim; "bodacious" is one that comes to mind. He would also have wanted to know what his cut would be and would have used his shotgun to ward off construction people until he got it. The building's corner units have the benefit of triangular bays of windows, giving residents views of the lake in three directions.

600 North Michigan Avenue
Beyer Blinder Belle of New York, 1997

This structure on the northwest corner of Ohio and Michigan serves as a store and a multi-screen cinema. The latter is on the top floors and requires a long escalator ride up from the entrance on Rush and Ohio. The building, while eye-catching, has been accused of not measuring up to Michigan Avenue in the twenty-first century. In *The Architecture of Chicago's Loop* (Sigma Press, 1998), Frances Steiner writes:

> The geometry of its profile, due especially to the rectangular cinema structure on top, weakens the appearance of the whole. The structure has aroused much controversy . . . because its character is in opposition to the elegant structures nearby.

American Medical Association Building
515 North State Street
Kenzo Tange with Shaw and Associates, 1990.

This 29-story building on the Near North Side is interesting and playful. The corner facing southwest has been flattened to help create a dramatic

Blue Cross–Blue Shield Building, as seen from Grant Park (Architect: Lohan Associates; Photographer: © Steinkamp/Ballogg, Chicago)

entrance to a grassy public plaza. Even more imaginative is a large *openway,* or spatial tunnel, that cuts through four floors near the top of the building.

Arts Club
211 East Ontario Street
Vinci/Hamp Architects, 1997

The old Arts Club was in an historic, charming building at 109 East Ontario Street. When it was to be razed and replaced by a new structure, the question was what to do with the 1951 Mies von der Rohe stairway. The solution was simple: move the staircase to the site of the new Arts Club and build around it.

Blue Cross–Blue Shield Building
300 East Randolph Street
Lohan Associates, 1996

This massive structure abutting Grant Park is 30 stories high and constructed so that, if needed, 24 more stories could be added later. It is a simple structure of glass and steel, but no less beautiful because of it.

Chicago Bar Association
321 South Plymouth Court
Tigerman/McCurry, 1990

The students at John Marshall Law School just to the north somehow survived the noise of this building's construction. A cast aluminum statue of Justice is perched above the entranceway of this 16-story structure designed to complement its neighbors on this quaint South Loop street.

Chicago Place
700 North Michigan Avenue
Skidmore, Owings & Merrill, 1990
Tower apartments: *Solomon Cordell Buenz & Associates*

Chicago Place itself faces Michigan Avenue and represents a commercial venture with verve. It was inspired, according to its architect, by Louis Sullivan's Carson Pirie & Scott store on Michigan Avenue. Inside, thanks to its glass elevators and long escalator ride, the visitor gets a glimpse of the various stores and, out of the eighth floor window, a view of Michigan Avenue.

Condo apartments fill up the rest of 40-floor structure. Through bay windows on the east and west sides, some residences afford people quite a panorama of the city, letting them look out in all four directions.

Chicago Title Tower
161–171 North Clark Street
Kohn Pederson Fox, 1992

This structure, named after the Chicago Title and Trust Company, which it houses, encourages the curious eye to scan 50 stories upward and appreciate the effect created by aluminum and white granite from Sardinia. The 13-story base is comparable in height to the nearby City Hall–County Building. It suffers, however, from being squeezed into the middle of a block and being across the street from the startling James R. Thompson (State of Illinois) Center.

City Place
676 North Michigan Avenue
Loebl, Schlossman & Hackl, 1990

Blue glass, red granite, an arch and setbacks contribute to the distinct appearance of this building which houses Michigan Avenue stores, a Huron Street hotel (a 25-story Hyatt Regency) and a 14-story office unit.

Cityfront Place
400–480 North McClurg Court
Gelick Foran Associates Ltd., 1992

This complex consists of a 39-story tower and two adjoining 12-story structures. The three buildings house 904 luxury apartments. Red brick cladding associates it with the original brick appearance of the North Pier Terminal to the east.

Crate & Barrel
646 North Michigan Avenue
Solomon Cordell Buenz & Associates, 1990

Experiencing this innovative housewares store can be at least a little comparable to walking into Sullivan's Schlesinger & Mayer department store 100 years ago. The five-floor building is designed to entice the potential

customer. The structure is basically a warehouse, but the walls are windows and the passersby can see the products, people and action from outside.

Gleacher Center of the University of Chicago (Architect: Lohan Associates; Photographer: Hedrich Blessing)

Gleacher Center of the University of Chicago

450 North Cityfront Plaza
Lohan Associates, 1994

A person may need a map to find this one, located on the river behind the Equitable Building, but it is worth the trip. As in a number of 1990s buildings, numerous rows of windows open up the Gleacher Center to

Museum of Contemporary Art

those curious about what goes on within its walls. The people inside are studying, hearing lectures or purchasing books at the U. of C. store. The building seems massive, without actually being very large; almost classical, but with a layered look that Frances Steiner, author of *The Architecture of Chicago's Loop,* saw as "relating to Deconstructivism." The Lohan Associates architect who worked on the building shook his head and laughed at the comment, however.

Harold Washington Library Center
400 South State Street
Hammond, Beeby & Babka, 1991

This 10-story structure houses the main branch of the Chicago public library, and fills a block just south of the Loop. Its design is an interesting variation on Sullivan's legendary Transportation Building design, which some historians believe marked the birth of modern architecture. Named after Mayor Harold Washington, who loved to read, the library building is indeed functional, except that it forces patrons to use the third rather than the first floor to check in or out. Then there are the giant gargoyles looking down from the roof—at them, the father of modern architecture would have stood aghast!

Heller International Tower
500 West Monroe Street
Skidmore, Owings & Merrill, 1992

The style of this massive structure west of the river seems a combination of that of the 1929 Civic Opera House a few blocks away, and the *Art Deco* look of the NBC Tower (1988). Neither the Heller nor the NBC structure need apologize that they both reflect the most famous building never built, Eliel Saarinen's entry that finished second in the 1922 contest to design the *Chicago Tribune* building.

McCormick Place South
2301 South Martin Luther King Drive
Thompson Ventulett Stainback & Associates;
A. Epstein & Sons International, 1997

This structure reminds one of a factory made entirely out of glass, with a cocky and strange hat for a roof. While a critical viewer might wish he or she could have gotten hold of the plans and made a suggestion or two, it is creative and comfortable, and it works, so forget the blue pencil.

The Museum of Contemporary Art
220 East Chicago Avenue
Joseph Paul Kleihues, 1996

Here is a building to love and respect, because it is both daring and successful. Some critics, however, do not like its looks. The design of the building is organic enough to be grasped as a whole, but also intricate. Steel spikes used in creating the building were left uncovered to emphasize rather than to hide the processes of construction. The architect deliberately chose materials that would age with time and that would let the appearance of the outside of the structure change with the faces of the city. A grand staircase from the lobby is a gasping discovery. Its wide spiral upward embodies the beauty and drama that one has a right to expect in the exhibits throughout the building.

North Pier Apartment Tower
474 North Lake Shore Drive
Dubin, Dubin & Moutoussamy and *Florian/Wierzbowski,* 1990

If this 61-story apartment building were in almost any other city, it would
be better known than it is in Chicago. The architects' use of five different
colors, as well as its size (505 apartment units) and location (at the junc-
tion of the lake and the river) make it noteworthy, but few Chicagoans
seem to have ever heard of it.

Paine Webber Tower
181 West Madison Street
Cesar Pelli, 1990

Like the Heller International Tower, this 51-story skyscraper was inspired
by Eliel Saarinen's entry in the 1922 Tribune Competition. It was in that
blueprint that staggered or *setback* construction was shown to be a thing
of beauty—as it is in the Paine Webber Tower. Years ago, massive buildings such as this, with their large, vaulted entranceways, were not used for
offices; instead, they frequently served as train depots. Such a structure is
meant to inspire the viewer with a sense of romance and adventure.

Ralph Metcalfe Federal Building
77 West Jackson Boulevard
Fujikawa, Johnson & Associates, 1992

The southeast section of the Loop is home to a cluster of federal buildings, which complement one another and yet remain individual. This
structure, which fills a full block, was designed by the two architects who
had served with Mies van der Rohe's firm, and his influence is apparent in
this work. Unlike in Mies's buildings, however, the windows are up against
the surface rather than between piers. The late Ralph Metcalfe, after
whom the building was named, was an Olympic runner, a Chicago alderman and finally a member of the U.S. House of Representatives.

Savings of America Tower
120 North LaSalle Street
Murphy/Jahn, 1991

If a Chicagoan wants to select five or ten of the newer buildings in the
Loop to show off to visitors, this should be one of them. It was created by

Helmut Jahn, who also designed the James R. Thompson Center. The tower is a 38-story, narrow, mid-block structure of granite and glass. Jahn used innovative forms and tall, straight lines to help the viewer's eye climb it visually. He crowned it with arch-shaped rooms at its summit. A large blue and gold mosaic by Roger Brown titled "The Flight of Daedalus and Icarus" hangs above the front entrance.

Sheraton Chicago Hotel and Towers
301 North Water Street
Solomon Cordwell Buenz & Associates, 1992

This riverside hotel features the city's largest ballroom, which covers an entire acre. It has 1200 guest rooms on 33 L-shaped floors. Three adjacent buildings have been added. They are a 30-story tower and two 12-story buildings that offer rental apartments.

23. Places of WORSHIP and BEAUTY: WHAT CHICAGOLAND HAS TO OFFER

The peace of great churches be for you . . .

—CARL SANDBURG

The remnants of ancient civilizations are often distinguished by temples and churches—the cathedrals of Europe; the Greek temple to Athena; the ashes of prehistoric home altars on the islands of the Mediterranean. From them archaeologists learn about not only people's relationship with the divine, but also their relationship with each other.

When people of the future reflect on the remains of *our* civilization, they will no doubt be struck by the unique diversity of the Unites States' places of worship. A vast variety of faiths have built here, with a feeling of religious intensity, a sense of ethnic pride and an eye for beauty.

The Chicago region offers as astounding an example of this diversity as any area in the country. The following list of ten beautiful places of worship pays homage to the variety of religious experiences that Chicagoland has embraced—and the freedom of religion that this diversity exemplifies:

1. Holy Trinity Russian Orthodox Cathedral

1121 North Leavitt Street, Chicago.

In the 1890s, with initial funding from Tsar Nicholas II, the Russian Orthodox community of Chicago started discussing the building of a church. The original plans called for a grandiose structure modeled after those of St. Petersburg and Moscow.

A switch of architects brought in Louis Sullivan, and along with him the dream of erecting a building in tune with the heritage of local Russian immigrants. Most of them were from more rural areas, where wooden churches expressed their simple faith.

Sullivan wanted to create functional architecture rather than designs which engendered awe. He looked to men's minds and hearts for his forms, rather than the elaborate models of the past. He was the ideal man for the task.

The cathedral was completed in 1903.

The Commission on Chicago Historical and Architectural Landmarks brochure says of it:

> Sullivan . . . was enthusiastic about his work and the relationship with the Russian community. He was so anxious that the church be completed as the parish envisioned that he returned half of his fee to the church in order that the decoration could be completed.

2. Baha'i House of Worship

Sheridan Road and Linden Avenue, Wilmette.

Architecture can afford to be intricate as long as it remains uncluttered and direct in execution. No structure in the Chicago area better demonstrates

SULLIVAN'S VISION

In a letter, Louis Sullivan wrote that he hoped Holy Trinity Russian Orthodox Cathedral would become one of the "the most unique and poetic buildings in the country." His wish was fulfilled.

Baha'i Temple in Wilmette (©1995 Dennis McClendon/ Chicago Carto-Graphics

this than the Baha'i Temple in Wilmette. Inside one finds no altar, pictures, candles or religious artifacts.

A sense of oneness, rather than a factional dogmatic creed, is the fundamental teaching of Baha'i's founder, Bahau'llah. Nine is the largest single-digit number, and Bahau'llah's followers see it as a symbol of this unity. So nine alcoves provide entrance to the building, and written above each is a quotation from Bahau'llah.

The Baha'i temple features more than 19,000 square feet of glass. Because of the many windows and the shape of the building, a person can look out from any place within it and see either Lake Michigan or the surrounding flower gardens.

The structure, open to visitors, was begun in 1920, but not completed until 1953.

3. Unity Temple

Lake Street at Kenilworth Avenue, Oak Park.

The Unitarian Universalist Church and Parish House (Unity Temple) was created by Frank Lloyd Wright in 1906. His design was bold and cubistic, the first of its kind. Wright formed the temple out of concrete, which was not only revolutionary but also allowed him to stay within the low budget for building the two conjoined structures.

The interior of the century-old temple is even more "modern" than the outside. The windows are among the best of Wright's abstract stained glass designs. The effects of both the furniture and the skylights are dramatic—and at the same time practical and spiritual. The insides of the buildings, their lighting and coloration, have been painstakingly restored to their original beauty.

4. Second Presbyterian Church

1936 South Michigan Avenue, Chicago.

This church was designed in 1874, three years after the Chicago Fire destroyed its predecessor, the so-called "spotted" church. The architect for the new building was James Renwick, who had created St. Patrick's Cathedral in New York.

The church was again injured by a fire in 1900 and then remodeled by Howard Van Doren Shaw. One can see his touches in the ceiling and rectangular windows just beneath the roof, which he had lowered. Shaw also designed the church's Arts and Crafts stained glass window, and added murals by Chicago artist Clay Bartlett.

The glory of the church, however, is in its seven stained glass windows by Louis Tiffany, designed between 1890 and 1919, the oldest being the Peace Window.

Second Presbyterian is a monument not only to God, but also to the neighborhood, which once included the Prairie Avenue mansions of Chicago's wealthiest citizens.

5. The Hindu Temple of Greater Chicago

10915 Lemont Road, Lemont.

Hindus believe that a temple building is itself a living organism and a form of God. Thus, the attention and devotion with which it is constructed and cared for is not surprising.

The Hindu Temple of Greater Chicago complex consists of two buildings, the Rama and the Ganesha-Shiva-Druga temples. Each was designed and constructed by artisans and sculptors who, like most of the people who worship here, were from India.

A sense of mystical respect settles on the visitor as he or she passes through the gate on Lemont Road. The property, situated in an area of hills and natural wildness found nowhere else in the Chicago area, offers a stunning view of the Des Plaines River Valley.

The gate to the grounds is flanked by three sets of tall columns, intricately carved to match the style of the Rama temple. The road winds up toward the complex, passing a large, dramatic statue of Lord Rama.

The two temples, temporarily marred by continuing construction efforts, nevertheless can inspire awe in those who approach them. It is not difficult to envision a future in which their beauty is more complete and settled.

The Rama temple authentically recreates the architectural style of tenth century Chola dynasty. It includes an 80-foot tower as a "potent" symbol of the Hindu spirit.

The Ganesha-Shiva-Durga temple was constructed in the architectural style of the first century Kalinga dynasty.

Before a person enters either temple, he or she respects the tradition of removing one's shoes. A low, hard bell can be rung by the arriving visitor or

worshipper. Each of the structures provides uniquely designed side rooms or temples in which people eat, pray, meditate and perform rituals to specific gods and goddesses.

A sign at the Rama temple announces that Ashtotara Archana will be performed every half hour. The ritual consists of pronouncing the 108 names of God.

6. Chicago Sinai Congregation and North Shore Congregation Israel

Chicago Sinai Congregation
15 West Delaware Place, Chicago.

Sinai Congregation, founded in 1861, was the first reform community in Chicago. Over the years its members met in various different synagogues, including one designed by Louis Sullivan and another created by the man who had been the architect of the Shedd Aquarium.

When the members decided to have a new house of worship constructed on the Near North Side, they first worked with an architect to explore conceptual ideas and perform feasibility studies. After ten years of study, the congregation sponsored an international design competition and, as a result, selected Lohan Associates to lead the project.

The new synagogue, completed in 1995, met Congregation Sinai's goal of "artistic distinction in a city famous for its architectural heritage."

Photos do not do justice to Chicago Sinai Congregation because it is difficult to find an angle from which to photograph it.

Is it new or is it old? It appears to be both.

The beauty of this temple, packed neatly into its Near North side location off State Street, is partially that its architecture seems to stand suspended in time. An individual can find in this synagogue the same ambiance and timelessness as in Louis Sullivan's works.

North Shore Congregation Israel
1185 Sheridan Road, Glencoe.

North Shore Congregation Israel's impact comes from its lines, which feel graceful, light and imaginative.

The arches that ascend the outside of the building are symbolic of hands at prayer. The fingers of these hands point to a roof with beautiful skylights that flood the body of the synagogue with light.

The sweeping lines of North Shore Israel are among the most dramatic and beautiful of any work of architecture in the Chicago area.

It was built from 1962 to 1964 and designed by Minoru Yamasaki along with the firm of Friedman, Alschuler and Sincere. Yamasaki is Japanese, while Friedman, Alschuler and Sincere are a firm with a long history of designing synagogues in Chicago.

7. St. Paul Catholic Church

2127 West 22nd Place, Chicago.

Over the years, architects of Chicago churches have often attempted to imitate the cathedrals and great churches of Europe. But rarely did they succeed in attaining the degree of beauty and dignity they sought. Many hundred-or-more–year–old churches throughout Chicago are a testament to this unfortunate fact.

BELIEVE IT OR NOT . . .

St. Paul Church was built without the use of a nail, a fact cited in a *Ripley's Believe It or Not* column.

Once in a great while, however, a structure comes close to capturing the essence of the European originals. This is the high accolade that one can give to the Gothic St. Paul Church and its architect, Henry Schlacks.

Working in the late 1890s, Schlacks called on the German workmen of the parish. They constructed their own church, just as local craftsmen had done in Europe in the Middle Ages.

Today, the parish serves members of a different ethnic community. The overlay of Hispanic religious symbols in a church built by its former German parishioners seems to have been achieved without conflict.

In their book *Chicago Churches and Synagogues,* Rev. George Lane, S. J. and Rev. Algimantas Kezys call St. Paul "a symphony in brick" and "distinctive for its beauty, proportions and engineering."

8. Elijah Muhammed Mosque #2

7351 South Stony Island Avenue, Chicago.

Chicago has long had a tradition when a new racial or ethnic group moves into an area in which it had not previously had a large presence: this new group's predominant religion takes over a house of worship constructed by members of a different ethnic group and religion. For example, the Chicago Sinai Congregation's first synagogue on Monroe between Clark and LaSalle Streets had been the Trinity Episcopal Church in the mid-1800s.

The large Nation of Islam mosque on South Stony Island was once SS. Constantine and Helen, the largest Greek Orthodox church in the Western Hemisphere. The building is modeled after the Church of St. Sophia in Constantinople.

The mosque represents an attractive use of limestone and straight and curved lines. It is dignified and vast, yet simple.

9. Seventeenth Church of Christ, Scientist

55 East Wacker Drive, Chicago.

Functionalism may be gospel in Chicago architecture, but it is not always easy to attain. This church certainly does, however. Located amid skyscrapers on a spare piece of land along the river at Wabash and Wacker, it has to fight both its location and the height of the buildings around it to be noticed and serve its purpose.

The attractive church, designed by Harry Weese and Associates in 1968, was created with reinforced concrete and uses semi-circular, ascending rows of seats to permit the Christian Scientist reader to address the audience.

The design of the Seventeenth Church of Christ, Scientist allows light into the lower-level section in which Sunday school is held, and keeps out the noise of the heavy traffic around the church.

WHY SO MANY DOMES?

St. Joseph Ukrainian Catholic Church has 13 domes, with the twelve small ones presenting the apostles and the center one symbolizing Christ. An extraordinary use of glass allows in an abundance of light.

10. St. Joseph Ukrainian Catholic Church

5000 North Cumberland Avenue, Chicago.

At first glance, this 1977 church, designed by Zenon Mazurkevich, looks to a Midwesterner as though it belongs on the set of a science-fiction movie. (With its friendliness and openness, however, it would certainly belong to the good guys of the film.) A second look, however, inspires reverence.

St. Joseph's location on the Northwest Side of Chicago finds it surrounded by traffic and homes. There is a humility to the setting of the church and a simplicity to the concrete with which it was constructed. They help make the structure particularly appropriate as a place of worship.

24. Beauty and Originality in the ARTS: 100 EVENTS FROM CHICAGO'S CULTURAL HISTORY

It is given to some cities, as to some lands, to suggest romance, and to me Chicago did that hourly. It sang, I thought . . . and I was singing with it.

—THEODORE DREISER, *A BOOK ABOUT MYSELF*

1. A native of the Chicago area, sometime in the period of unrecorded history between 1400 and 1500 AD, carved a unique piece of art, a gorget mask.

   Sculpted on a seashell, this item of ornamental jewelry is in the likeness of a face, with lines etched as paths for tears. Some 400 to 500 years later, archaeologists would uncover it lying on the chest of skeletal remains at the Anker Site in Thornton Township on the Little Calumet River. The dig was started on the Anker farm because a subdivision was to be built there.

2. Jean Baptiste Point DuSable brought western culture and art to the Chicago area in the 1780s, constructing a home, an extensive farm and a trading post at the mouth of the Chicago River.

   His possessions, which would be listed in a bill of sale in 1800, included such items as a horse mill, a bakehouse, a large number of tools, poultry, cattle, mules and furniture. Astoundingly, deep in a wilderness hundreds of miles from any roads, he also owned "several paintings."

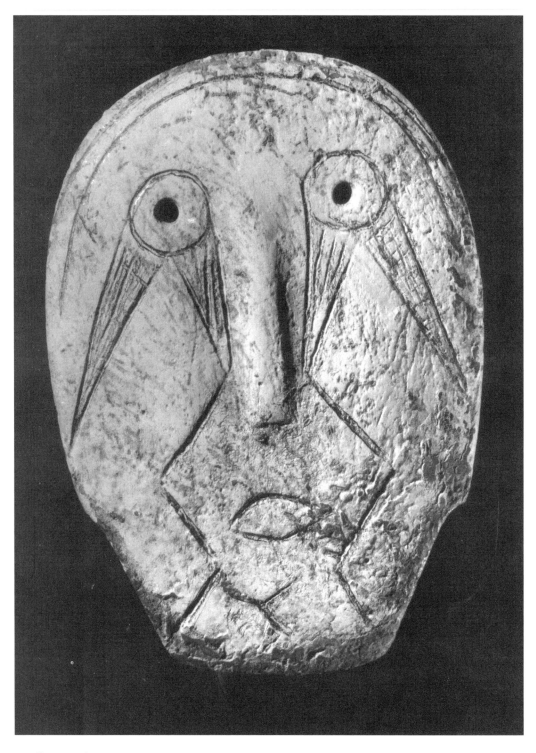

Gorget mask,
circa 1400 or
1500 AD

Kinzie Mansion, formerly the home of Jean Baptiste and Catherine Point DuSable (Author's collection)

3. In 1833, Chicago, a village with a population of only 300, witnessed an architectural first: "balloon frame" construction.

This efficient new building design incorporated lightweight, machine-crafted materials, and would be used to erect the residences and commercial buildings needed on the prairies of what was then called "the West." The construction technique's first recorded use was for St. Mary's Catholic Church on the southwest corner of Lake and State Streets.

4. In 1850, portrait artist George P. A. Healy arrived in Chicago.

The rough frontier town had a population of only 28,269. Nevertheless, Healey honored the request of former mayor William Ogden, and left the royal court of France to come to the small frontier town. His acclaimed works celebrate the prominent Chicagoans who served as the subjects of his brush.

5. *Chicago Magazine: The West As It Is Illustrated* was published in 1857.

At this point, the railroads had just come to Chicago and population was soaring past the 100,000 mark. Zeb Eastman and a group of

Chicagoans produced this monthly publication to show the town's brief history and serve as a forum for its budding literary efforts. Unfortunately, a recession hit the city soon thereafter, and limited their publication to five memorable issues.

6. **In 1860, Chicagoan Leonard W. Volk sculpted his famous bust of Abraham Lincoln.**

His work won recognition across the country during the presidential campaign, and later became famous throughout the world. His influence lives on in Chicago—in 1887, Augustus Saint-Gaudens used it as a model for his Standing Lincoln sculpture, which presides over Lincoln Park to this day. Many consider this piece to be the noblest portrait statue in the nation.

7. **From 1861 to 1865, Chicago served as the music-making "Tin Pan Alley" of the Civil War.**

From Chicago firm Root & Cady came such patriotic songs as "Tramp, Tramp, Tramp" and "Kingdom Coming." Its most popular song, "The Battle Cry of Freedom," contained the line, "We'll rally round the flag, boys," epitomizing and fueling the burst of patriotic fervor that helped the North win the Civil War.

8. **In 1879, Frances Willard was elected president of the Woman's Christian Temperance Union in Evanston, a position she would use to lead the fights both against alcohol and for women's suffrage.**

Her voice as an orator, educator, newspaper editor, author and national figure aroused women's interest in the world around them. Her books, noted for their directness and eloquence, would urge women to fight for the right to enter the many professions from which they were excluded.

9. **Francis Fisher Browne founded *The Dial* magazine in 1880 and initiated Chicago's long-standing reputation for literary criticism.**

His publication was described by a contemporary as "the most unbiased, good-humored organ of American criticism." It would last 38 years, longer than any similar publication of its era.

10. In 1883, Eugene Field joined Victor Lawson's *Morning News* as a columnist.

The puckish journalist and poet built readership and a national reputation by poking fun at the fatuous culture of the East Coast and the pork belly one in Chicago. He also wrote wonderful children's poems such as "Little Boy Blue" and "Wynken, Blynken and Nod."

11. In 1885, Architect William Le Baron Jenney completed the world's first skyscraper, the Home Insurance Building at LaSalle and Adams Streets.

The structure, 10 stories high with two more to be added later, was the first to meet the definition of a skyscraper—it relied on a metal skeleton rather than the outside walls to bear its weight. This new construction method forever changed the look and lines of tall commercial structures throughout the world. Louis Sullivan apprenticed in Jenney's firm.

12. The Newberry Library, temporarily housed at 90 LaSalle Street, opened its doors to the public September 6, 1887.

The last will of Chicago real estate magnate Walter Newberry had taken effect after the deaths of his daughters and wife. Its provisions had called for the creation of "a free public library" in the city. The Newberry moved to its own building in 1893. Concentrating on history, maps, genealogy and the humanities, it has become one of the world's great research libraries.

13. The John J. Glessner family moved into its new home on Prairie Avenue on December 1, 1887.

Its architect, Henry Hobson Richardson, did not live to see the completed structure at 1800 South Prairie Avenue. He died five days after finishing the drawings. By dramatically rejecting the traditional architectural forms for innovative and more practical ideas, this house is generally believed to have changed residential construction for all time.

14. In 1888, Frank Lloyd Wright, a young aspiring draftsman from Wisconsin, joined the architectural firm of Adler and Sullivan, whom he would later call "the great moderns."

Shortly thereafter, in 1891, his designs for the Charnley House on North Astor Street would foreshadow his enormous future as an innovative residential architect. Two years later, he set out on his own. His Prairie School architectural style became the basis for twentieth century design of living space.

15. **In 1888, John Wellborn Root and Daniel Burnham's Rookery Building was completed.**

It not only stands as one of the most beautiful commercial structures of all times, but also set the standards for office size, corridor width and placement of elevators in commercial buildings for the next 50 years.

16. **U.S. President Benjamin Harrison dedicated the Auditorium December 9, 1889.**

Louis Sullivan and Dankmar Adler had created the greatest opera house in the world, one that could seat 4,000 with room for another 3,000 on special occasions. Its extraordinary acoustics eliminated the echoes of other music halls and theaters, while its democratic seating plans eschewed the boxes for the wealthy found in the Metropolitan Opera House in New York, and elsewhere.

17. **In 1889, Jane Addams and Ellen Gates Starr established Hull House in an old mansion at Halsted and Polk Streets.**

It served immigrants and the poor of Chicago, respecting each person's individuality and dignity in doing so. For generations, its programs afforded the underprivileged the opportunities denied them by society. Addams eventually became, according to the polls, the most respected woman in America. In 1930 she shared the Nobel Peace Prize.

18. **The Chicago Symphony Orchestra performed its first concert on October 16, 1891.**

Chicago utilities executive Charles Norman Fay had invited conductor Theodore Thomas, "America's musical missionary," to build a residential orchestra for the city. The latter responded with the famous line, "I would go to hell if they would give me a permanent orchestra." He recruited 86 musicians (60 of them from New York) to create the CSO. Its first home was in the Auditorium. On the premiere program was Tchaikovsky's First Piano Concerto.

Golden Door of the Transportation Building at the 1893 World's Fair (Author's collection)

19. The University of Chicago was founded in 1891.

It was built on ten acres in the Hyde Park neighborhood donated by Marshall Field, with $600,000 contributed by John D. Rockefeller. The scholastic standards, ideals and vision, however, belonged to its president, William Rainey Harper. His ambition was to create a true university because he believed that "A college teaches, but a university teaches—and also learns."

20. At Chicago's World's Columbian Exposition of 1893, the design of one structure, Louis Sullivan and Dankmar Adler's Transportation Building, represented a radical change in architectural design.

Historians have acclaimed it as the beginning of modern architecture. Sullivan's "form follows function" philosophy contrasted with a long history throughout the Western world of classical and neoclassical design.

21. At the 1893 World's Fair, an exhibit of French Impressionist paintings loaned by Bertha Palmer startled the art establishment.

At this point, many art enthusiasts still considered the Impressionists to be artistic anarchists and revolutionaries. Pittsburgh multimillionaire

Andrew Carnegie had called on the wealthy of America to boycott them. Mrs. Palmer, meanwhile, was accumulating works by Renoir, Degas, Monet, Corot, Delacroix, Pissaro and Sissley.

22. In 1893, Herbert Stone and Hannibal Kimball founded Stone & Kimball, one of the most original and creative publishing companies of the era.

The two young Chicagoans, both in their early 20s, produced esthetically designed first editions, and a respected and popular literary magazine, the *ChapBook*. The authors whom they would publish included Robert Louis Stevenson, George Bernard Shaw, Eugene Field, George Ade, Mary MacLane, George Barr McCutcheon, Henry James and Elia Peattie.

23. In 1894, William T. Stead published the book *If Christ Came to Chicago,* a profound analysis of the city, what it was and might become.

Chicago was stunned. The visiting British journalist and reformer had exposed graft and City Council "boodling" in detail, naming the individuals he held responsible. He also criticized "the Chicagoan trinity" of Marshall Field, Philip D. Armour and George Pullman, while praising Jane Addams and mapping out a plan "for all who love in the service of all who suffer." The first printing of the book sold more than 100,000 copies, and the work became recognized as a classic in urban literature.

24. In 1897, Finley Peter Dunne started writing his "Mr. Dooley" columns in the *Chicago Journal* and gave American literature one of its most distinctive characters.

The loquacious Mr. Dooley, "Archey Road" Irish saloon keeper, provided Chicagoans and later the country with such insightful comments as "Trust ivrybody, but cut th' ca-ards" and "I care not who makes th' laws if I can get out an injunction." His creator also would play a key role in the Anti-Imperialist League's campaign against this country's war in the Philippines.

25. Chicago formed the first U.S. chapter of the Arts & Crafts Society in 1897.

This movement represented an intense effort to create and appreciate handcrafted artifacts rather than machine-made ones, and enrolled architects, artists, instructors, professors, professional craftsmen, hobbyists and homemakers. Among its greatest proponents were Frank Lloyd Wright, Louis Sullivan and the women of Hull House. Sears Roebuck & Company and the Montgomery Ward Company catalogues helped popularize the movement by selling furniture and other items produced by its members.

26. In 1899, University of Chicago Professor Thorstein Veblen published a classic critique of modern culture, *The Theory of the Leisure Class.*

Rich in evidence, analysis and irony, the book outlines the important distinctions between those who make things and those who purchase them. The impact of this volume continued to grow in the twentieth century—some of its phrases, such as "conspicuous consumption," have become part of the American vocabulary.

27. John Dewey published *School and Society: The School and Social Progress* in 1900.

His book called for teachers and school authorities to educate rather than indoctrinate. The University of Chicago educator and philosopher shares with Chicagoan Francis Parker the title of Father of Progressive Education.

28. In 1900, former Chicago journalist L. Frank Baum and local artist William W. Denslow offered the world an American fairy tale, *The Wonderful Wizard of Oz.*

Children loved the book so much that they importuned Baum to write sequels. The artwork of William W. Denslow helped make it one of the truly beautiful books in American publishing history. *The Wizard of Oz* would become a play in 1902 and, in 1939, one of the most famous movies ever made.

29. The breakthrough novel *Sister Carrie* was published in 1900.

Its author, Theodore Dreiser, tells of how Caroline "Carrie" Meeber arrives in Chicago, makes a life for herself in the city, and gets caught in the whirlwind of city life. She faces and adopts a whole different moral code than the one discussed in rural America or written about in the literature of the time. In this novel, the "wayward" protagonist is not punished for her "sins."

30. Walt Disney was born Dec. 5, 1901 in a modest Chicago home at 1249 Tripp Street.

Attending McKinley High School, he would contribute to the school paper a number of drawings that would augur his future career as an artist. With the help of the company he founded, this one-man force in American entertainment would create or set in motion Mickey Mouse, *Snow White, Fantasia, The Mickey Mouse Club,* Disneyland and the Disney Channel.

31. Ravinia Park opened its gates to the public on August 15, 1904.

The Highland Park outdoor theater would become internationally acclaimed for its music festivals and as the summer home for the Chicago Symphony Orchestra. Its fresh air performances over the years have included pop music, opera series and performances by the top musicians in the world. To many Chicagoans, picnics there before a program have long been a summer must.

32. In 1906, Upton Sinclair published his exposé novel *The Jungle.*

The book centered on the lives of the immigrant Chicago stockyards workers and the injustices they suffered. It was also a major exposé of the dangerous and unsanitary practices of the meat industry. This major classic has been reproduced in more than 1,000 editions and reprinted throughout the world.

33. In 1909, the Commercial Club published *The Plan of Chicago* by Daniel Burnham and Edward Bennett.

Within a few years, hundreds of other cities around the country would imitate Chicago and develop their own plans for urban beautification.

34. Chicago opera diva Mary Garden performed *Salome* in 1910.

The critics were split. After listening to her sing and watching her do the Dance of the Seven Veils, *Chicago Tribune* drama writer Percy Hammond, called her "the feminine colossus who doth bestride our operatic world."

Police chief LeRoy Steward, however, commented: "It was disgusting. Miss Garden wallowed around like a cat in a bed of catnip."

35. In October 1912, Harriet Monroe and her staff published the first issue of *Poetry: A Magazine of Verse*.

An office on Cass Street was headquarters for this small but ambitious publication. Early issues would include the poems of Ezra Pound, T. S. Eliot, Amy Lowell, Sara Teasdale, Nicholas Vachel Lindsay, Edgar Lee Masters, Joyce Kilmer and Carl Sandburg. Almost a century later, it is still going strong.

36. In November 1912, Maurice and Ellen Browne used enthusiastic amateur actors in theatrical roles traditionally restricted to professionals, thus initiating what became known as the Little Theater Movement.

Their first performance, *The Trojan Women,* was presented on a stage in the Fine Arts Building. British playwright George Bernard Shaw would later speak of the relevance of this beginning, saying in retrospect, "The work 20 years ago on the flour floor in Chicago—that is what matters."

37. Film comedian Charlie Chaplin joined Essanay Studios on January 2, 1913.

A large warehouse at 1345 Argyle Street was the home of the nascent— and silent—movie industry in this country. Its film colony included such other actors as Francis X Bushman, Gloria Swanson, Ben Turpin, Colleen Moore and Tom Mix. The Essanay name came from the first letters of the last names of its two founders, George Spoor and E. A. Ahmet. After World War I, moviemaking headed west to Hollywood.

38. In 1914, Edgar Rice Burroughs authored *Tarzan of the Apes,* basing the novel on a short story he had written two years earlier.

A native of Chicago and long-time resident of Oak Park, he had never visited Africa any more than as a science-fiction writer he would ever be on the moon. This book, the first of 30 Tarzan titles, would be translated into 56 languages and made into radio shows, comics and movies.

39. In 1914, Chicago sports columnist Ring Lardner began writing his *Saturday Evening Post* stories about fictional rookie baseball pitcher Jack Keefe.

These took the form of letters back home and would later be compiled in the book *You Know Me, Al*. Their human insight and use of the language of ordinary people established Lardner as a uniquely American writer. He was a *Chicago Tribune* sports reporter and there initiated the column "In the Wake of the News."

40. Margaret Anderson founded *The Little Review* in 1914 and promised its pages would offer "untrammeled liberty."

Its issues would be full of original, often controversial articles. She would co-publish James Joyce's *Ulysses* and be convicted and fined for violating laws against pornography. In her autobiography, she would write, "My greatest enemy is reality. I have fought it successfully for years."

41. Edgar Lee Masters fascinated 1915 readers with his realistic but charming *Spoon River Anthology.*

This former law partner of Clarence Darrow presented the stories of people in a cemetery in Central Illinois. He let them tell their tales with an honesty about everyday life that Americans usually wanted swept under the carpet. The work was critically acclaimed as innovative and refreshing.

42. In 1915, Willa Cather wrote *The Song of the Lark,* one of the most lyrical novels ever set in Chicago.

It tells the story of a young woman, Thea Kronberg, who comes to the city to study opera and falls in love with a painting at the Art Institute of Chicago. In 1935, Cather would author *Lucy Gayheart,* a novel with a similar story. Both describe young women encountering the potentially rich fabric of urban life.

43. In March, 1916, Henry Holt & Co. issued Carl Sandburg's *Chicago Poems.*

Sandburg, a journalist and poet, and later a Lincoln biographer, used free verse style to express the pulse of the "city of the big shoulders" and create an image of the Windy City that would echo throughout the world and in hundreds of books about Chicago. He was, at the time, a reporter for the *Chicago Daily News* and often wrote his poems while watching silent films, which he reviewed for the newspaper.

44. The Dill Pickle Club, a forum for anyone with unorthodox views, opened in 1917 as a discussion group for pro-labor activists, Wobblies and other leftists.

It would move within a year to its famed Tooker Place address in the Gold Coast neighborhood. The legendary club lasted well into the 1920s and was a gathering place for free thinkers and a stage for "anyone who is a nut about something."

45. On October 28, 1917, the *Chicago Tribune* published an article by H. L. Mencken in which he called Chicago "the most civilized city in America" and culturally "alive from snout to tail."

Known as the pundit of Baltimore, Mencken was also the nation's foremost literary maven. He made his point in eloquent sentences

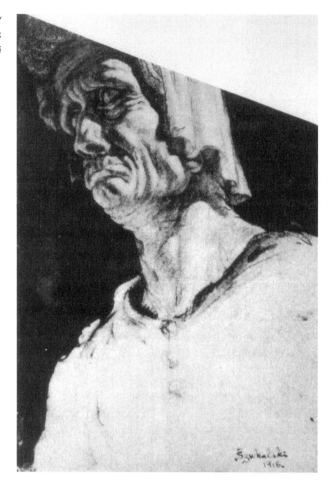

such as, "Find me a writer who is undoubtedly an American and who
has something new to say, and who says it with an air, and nine times
out of ten I will show that he has some sort of connection with the
abattoir by the lake."

**46. Chicago sculptor and painter Stanislaus Szukalski was given a one
man show in 1917 at the Art Institute.**

The trustees removed one of his paintings because they found it of-
fensive to the British, a World War I ally of the United States. The
artist reacted, knocking his own statues off their pedestals and
smashing the glass frames of his paintings. His art, Ben Hecht would
later say, was "like a new and violent people who had invaded the
earth."

122—Fountain of Time, Washington Park, Chicago

1920s postcard view of the Fountain of Time

47. Chicagoan Sherwood Anderson's novel *Winesburg, Ohio* was published in 1919.

Until then, his unpublished manuscripts had earned him a reputation as the city's best unpublished author. This American classic, set in a small Ohio town, shows characters devoted so singularly to a truth that it becomes a falsehood.

48. In 1922, Sculptor Loredo Taft's massive sculpture "The Fountain of Time" was unveiled.

Located in Washington Park at the west end of the Midway Plaisance, the statue group had taken 13 years to complete. Words on its base cite Austin Dobson's poem "The Paradox of Time": "Time goes, you say? Ah, no. Alas, time stays. We go." The thoughtful sculpture would remain into the next century, as would many of Taft's other efforts to enrich and beautify the Chicago area.

49. On June 10, 1922, the *Chicago Tribune* announced an international architectural competition to design its new Michigan Avenue building.

More than 300 architects contributed a total of 263 entries. A third of these were from other countries, thus commingling design ideas from throughout a world that had been split asunder by World War I. This

Early postcard view of the Tribune Tower

interbreeding of ideas helped propel commercial architecture dramatically forward.

50. *A Thousand and One Afternoons in Chicago* by journalist, poet and novelist Ben Hecht was published in 1922.

In these tales, which had first appeared in the *Chicago Daily News,* Hecht again demonstrated his skills as a masterful storyteller. Hollywood would eventually lay claim to his talents and he would become one of the most successful screenwriters in the history of motion pictures.

51. Louis "Satchmo" Armstrong arrived in Chicago in August 1922 to join King Oliver and His Creole Jazz Band.

The latter was led by Papa Joe "King" Oliver, Armstrong's former mentor in New Orleans. After Armstrong's first show with the group in the Lincoln Gardens on the South Side, the audience yelled out, "Let youngster blow." In his autobiography, he recalled his own feelings at the time: "I had hit the big time. I was up North with the greats."

52. Edna Ferber won the Pulitzer Prize in 1925 for her novel *So Big*.

The work is about Dutch immigrants in Chicago and the suburb of South Holland. Its characters, especially Dirk "So Big" DeJong, are

among the most distinctive of the era and of Chicago literature in general.

53. Clarence Darrow, known as the "attorney for the damned," defended two young thrill killers, Richard Loeb and Nathan Leopold, in 1924.

Darrow's eloquent, thoughtful words pleaded not only for their lives but also for a time "when we learn by reason and judgment and understanding and faith that all life is worth saving and that mercy is the highest attribute of man." The judge heard his mitigating arguments and sentenced the pair to "99 years plus life" rather than, as expected, to death.

54. In 1926, Frederic Clay Bartlett, a Chicago painter and patron of the arts, donated a collection of paintings to the Art Institute of Chicago that included *Sunday Afternoon on the Island of La Grande Jatte*.

Suerat's pointillist work is enjoyed and respected as one of the greatest drawings of the nineteenth century. Among the other pieces in the collection were Picasso's *The Old Guitarist,* Toulouse Lautrec's *At the Moulin Rouge,* Cézanne's *Basket of Apples,* Van Gogh's *Room at Arles,* Henri Rousseau's *The Waterfall,* Matisse's *Woman on a Rose Divan* and Gauguin's *The Day of the God.*

55. *The Front Page,* a play by Ben Hecht and Charlie MacArthur about Chicago journalism, opened in 1927.

The authors, expatriate Chicago reporters, explained in an "afterword" why they wrote it: "The inequities, double dealings, chicaneries and immoralities which as ex-Chicagoans we knew so well returned us to a mist called the Good Old Days, and our delight in our memories would not be denied." Three separate movies have been filmed based on their play.

56. Gospel music was born in Chicago in 1930, when Thomas Dorsey wrote for National Baptist Jubilee the song "If You See My Savior, Tell Him You Saw Me."

Some, however, have put gospel's birth date two years later, citing Dorsey's subsequent song, the immensely popular, "Precious Lord, Hold My Hand," which he wrote after the death of his wife. In gospel music Dorsey brought together blues rhythms and traditional African-American shout music. The musician-composer had previously performed with the ribald blues singer Ma Rainey

57. Chicagoan Margaret Ayer Barnes was awarded the 1931 Pulitzer Prize for her novel *Years of Grace*.

She had taken up writing while recuperating in a hospital after an automobile accident. In 1926 her sister, Janet Ayer Fairbanks, was announced as second in competition for the prize after Sinclair Lewis turned it down for his novel *Arrowsmith*.

58. Grant Wood, a former student at the Art Institute of Chicago, exhibited his painting *American Gothic* at the 1933 A Century of Progress Exhibition.

The individuals who posed for it in 1930 were his sister and a dentist friend. It was intended as a satire of German and Flemish artists, but has become instead a nostalgic symbol of America's past.

59. James T. Farrell published his breakthrough novel *Young Lonigan: A Boyhood in Chicago Streets* in 1932.

The dust jacket of this classic explains that its realism represents a form of sociology and should be understood as such. A young Irish South Sider, Studs Lonigan, is the tragic protagonist of this and two additional novels. All three books would later be published together as the *Studs Lonigan Trilogy*.

60. Archibald MacLeish, a native of Glencoe, won the Pulitzer in 1933 for his poem *Conquistador*.

He was the son of the president of Carson Pirie Scott & Co. After two years at New Trier High School in Winnetka, he had been shipped off to boarding school, which he hated. A Phi Beta Kappa from Yale, he was first in his law school class at Harvard. MacLeish would be awarded a second Pulitzer 1953 for his *Collected Poems* as well as one in drama in 1959 for *J.B.* He would also serve a stint as the librarian of Congress.

61. In 1933, Virginia Payne was heard on the soap opera *Ma Perkins* for the first time.

Ma Perkins and Virginia Payne would stay together for 27 years—7,065 shows. The Chicago-based daytime serials helped the city dominate the innovative new field of radio broadcasting, offering a range of programs from the broad humor of *Amos 'n' Andy* to the more sophisticated weekly half-hour drama *First Nighter*.

62. Chicagoan Benny Goodman first brought swing music to national attention in November 1935 during his band's engagement at the Chicago Congress Hotel.

Benny Goodman (JAMC Neg. 1033, Jane Addams Memorial Collection, special collection of the University Library, The University of Illinois at Chicago)

He created it by mixing the "swing" of black jazz with the sophisticated structures of classical music. It became the basis of the popular Big Band and dance music for the next couple of decades and gave Goodman the title "The King of Swing."

63. Christopher Morley, enraptured with the freshness and beauty of the city, captured it in his 1935 book *Old Loopy: A Love Letter for Chicago*.

In it, he wrote, "Everything about her [Chicago] has always contradicted the foretold and expected. She spikes the small beer of living with the pure alcohol of the impossible." To Morley, Chicago "has always seemed completely feminine."

Moholy = Nagy

EDITED BY RICHARD KOSTELANETZ
Documentary Monographs in Modern Art

64. In 1937, Laszlo Moholoy-Nagy founded the New Bauhaus design school in the old Field Mansion at 1905 South Prairie Avenue.

It did not succeed, but he tried again in 1939, opening the School of Design. The school would help change the course of artistic design in this country and, after his death in 1946, was integrated into the Illinois Institute of Technology. Among the many original ideas with which he worked were photomontages and functional typography.

65. Mies van der Rohe arrived in Chicago on October 18, 1938.

A recent immigrant from Nazi Germany and former head of the Bauhaus School of Design there, he had come to the city to become director of the school of architecture at the Armour Institute. The innovative architect proceeded to create a new, utilitarian glass-and-steel look for the skylines of the world.

66. In 1940, Richard Wright wrote the novel *Native Son,* an undisputed classic that would sell millions of copies.

The novel is the story of Bigger Thomas, trapped at the end of the tunnel of racism in the United States. *The New York Times* review said, "Native Son declares Richard Wright's importance, not merely as the best Negro writer, but as an American author as distinctive as any of those writing today."

67. In 1946, Chicago polka king Walter "Li'l Wally" Jagiello cut his first two records.

They were "Our Break Up" and "Away from Chicago." The polka, a Central European musical style which had been around more than a hundred years, was finding a new life and emanating not from Poland, but from Chicago and, to a lesser extent, places in Pennsylvania. Li'l Wally and other polka players such Frankie Yankovich, who had been packing Southwest Side and Milwaukee Avenue polka halls, began cutting records and became international stars.

68. The puppet show *Kukla, Fran & Ollie* first appeared on Chicago's WBKB-TV in 1947.

The Burr Tillstrom program, which featured such characters as Kukla, Ollie, Madame Ooglepuss, Beulah Witch, Colonel Crackie, etc., was a standout success and would last ten years. It was part of the pioneering "Chicago School" of live television that included *Studs' Place* (with Studs Terkel), *Garroway at Large, Walt's Workshop* and *Ding Dong School.*

69. In 1950, slide guitarist Muddy Waters exploded onto the national "downhome rythym and blues" scene with his first single on Chess Records.

Author Peter Guralnick would later write that Waters "deserves all the honorifics that have been bestowed on him: Father, Godfather, King of the Chicago Blues" and the Rolling Stones would take their name from one of his recordings. The Chess brothers, Leonard and Phil, proceeded to record almost every Chicago bluesman from Waters through the revolutionary Check Berry and Bo Diddley.

70. **Gwendolyn Brooks won the Pulitzer Prize for poetry in 1950 for** *Annie Allen.*

She had already been the recipient of six other literary awards and would be honored with more by the dozen before her death in 2000. She would write a novel, *Maud Martha* (1953), in addition to a wonderfully long list of poetry books including: *A Street in Bronzeville* (1945), *Bronzeville Boys and Girls* (1956), *The Bean Eaters* (1960), *Selected Poems* (1963), *In the Mecca* (1968), *Riot* (1969), *Family Pictures* (1970) and *The World of Gwendolyn Brooks* (1971). Borrowing a phrase from Ezra Pound, one writer would describe Brooks' poetry as "the antennae of the race"—in this case, the human race.

71. **The Art Institute of Chicago afforded photographer Harry Callahan a one-man show from April 23 to May 31, 1951.**

He then became head of the Department of Photography at the Institute of Design of the Illinois Institute of Technology. In a book published by the Museum of Modern Art, Sherman Paul would write of his photographs: "In this assimilation of advanced technique to subjectivity, in this concern for the education of artists, one recognizes the auspices of the New Vision, which brought back to Chicago its greatest heritage: the pragmatic-organic tradition of John Dewey and Louis Sullivan."

72. **In 1951, Nelson Algren penned** *Chicago: City on the Make,* **one of grittiest, most poetic tributes by a writer to his hometown.**

In it, he wrote, "Before you earn the right to rap any sort of joint, you have to love it a little while. You have to belong to Chicago like a cross-town transfer out of the Armitage Avenue barns first; and you can't rap it just because you've been cross-town." He had earlier received the National Book Award for his novel *A Walk on the Wild Side.*

73. Illinois governor Adlai Stevenson accepted the Democratic Party presidential nomination in a speech to the Democratic National Convention in Chicago on July 22, 1952.

He spoke elegantly, with the simple, direct tenor that had characterized Lincoln and would later characterize John F. Kennedy. "Let's talk sense to the American people," he told the convention. "Let's tell the truth that there are no gains without pains, that we are on the eve of great decisions, not easy decisions."

74. *Chicago's Left Bank,* written in 1953 by Alson J. Smith, celebrated the achievements of the city's creative force, calling Chicago, "Florence to New York's Rome" and "the fertile seedbed for a good part of the native culture of the United States."

The book contrasted sharply with A. J. Liebling's critical *New Yorker* series and 1952 book, *Chicago: The Second City,* in which he wrote that Chicago's contribution to American culture had "stopped as suddenly as a front-running horse at the head of the stretch with a poor man's two dollars on its nose."

75. Ernest Hemingway was announced as the winner of the 1954 Nobel Prize for Literature.

A native of Oak Park and copywriter for Firestone Tires in Chicago during the early 1920s, he subsequently moved to Paris. There, in his highly acclaimed novel *The Sun Also Rises,* he became known as the chronicler of "The Lost Generation." His later books included *A Farewell To Arms, For Whom the Bell Tolls* and *The Old Man and the Sea.* It was the latter that led to the Nobel Prize.

76. **Diva Maria Callas guest starred with the new Lyric Opera on November. 15, 1954.**

The role in which she had been cast was Lucia in *Lucia di Lammermoor.* Her stunning performance helped awaken the city's interest in the relatively new opera company. The *Chicago Daily News* reported, "The most exciting soprano in the world sang as she—or anybody else—may never have sung before and may never sing again." Another critic said her first act "spun like warm silk, sometimes with an edge of steel."

77. **Katherine Dunham, a onetime University of Chicago student, performed "primitive" and West Indian dancing at the Great Northern Theater in October 1955.**

Chicago American-dance critic Ann Barzel wrote of her performance, "She has been imitated extensively. Seeing the original makes one realize how pale and colorless the copies are. Miss Dunham's intellectual approach, her research in folk art have resulted in works that are more profoundly emotional than the superficial Calypso numbers that pop up on your TV screen and pep up too many night club shows."

78. **In December 1957, the Old Town School of Folk Music opened at 333 North Avenue, part of a folk-music tradition in Chicago that went back to the 1920s and Carl Sandburg's *American Songbook.***

Among the school's early students and teachers were Roger McGuinn of the Byrds, Bob Gibson, John Prine, Bonnie Koloc, Kristin Lems and the late Steve Goodman. By the end of the century enrollment had increased from 150 per week to more than 3,000.

79. **A new magazine, *Big Table I,* was issued March 17, 1959. It contained "beat generation" articles from the suppressed Winter 1958 issue of the University of Chicago student publication *Chicago Review.***

Among these articles were eight chapters of *Naked Lunch* by William S. Burroughs and a stream-of-consciousness meditation, *Old Angel*

CHICAGO TREASURES

Midnight, by Jack Kerouac. U. of C. chancellor Lawrence Kimpton had
learned of what the *Chicago Review* intended to publish and prohib-
ited it from doing so. Four months later, the *Review* editors brought
out *Big Table I.* The U.S. Post Office seized hundreds of copies for al-
leged pornography but eventually the publication was exonerated
when an attempt to prosecute its editors failed.

80. Lorraine Hansberry's *A Raisin in the Sun* opened in Chicago in January
1959 and then on Broadway on March 11.

It starred Sidney Poitier, Ruby Dee and Louis Gossett. This play, about
an African-American family trying to move into an all-white neighborhood, is partially autobiographical. The work received the New
York Drama Circle Award and is considered a precursor to the Civil
Rights statements of the 1960s.

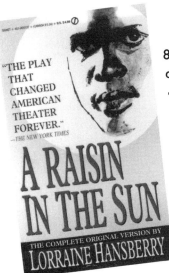

"THE PLAY THAT CHANGED AMERICAN THEATER FOREVER."
—THE NEW YORK TIMES

A RAISIN IN THE SUN

THE COMPLETE ORIGINAL VERSION BY
LORRAINE HANSBERRY

81. Improv theater was born as The Second City opened its doors on December 16, 1959 at 1842 North Wells Street.

The cast, which included Barbara Harris and Severn Darden, performed socially conscious skits and then improvised sketches based on suggestions from the audience, a formula the group still uses today. The Second City spawned the TV show *Saturday Night Live* and similar improv companies in other cities.

82. The Art Institute of Chicago honored painter Ivan Albright with a retrospective that ran from Oct. 30 through December 27, 1964.

His works have been called both "innovative" and "grotesque." He painted with an incomparable sense of the surfaces of things and people. Sculptor Jean Dubuffet wrote of him, "I do not believe that I have ever encountered a painting which gave me immediately such a sense of commotion as one by Ivan Albright portraying a door; I found it at the Art Institute during my brief stay in Chicago. It is an unforgettable painting, and it seems to me, a striking example of a work that is worth going to the ends of the earth to see."

83. Chicago's Picasso was unveiled on August 15, 1967.

Mayor Richard J. Daley dedicated the sculpture by 85-year-old Pablo Picasso in what is now Daley Plaza with "the belief that what is strange today will be familiar tomorrow." Indeed, this sculpture would justify his belief. The 50-foot, 162-ton work that launched a million jokes has become a symbol of the city. Such familiarity, the *Tribune's* Alan Artner has pointed out, can be "the first step toward love."

84. Georg Solti took the helm of the Chicago Symphony Orchestra in 1969.

In *Season with Solti*, William Barry Furlong wrote of the event: "Then came Solti—bald, intense, filled with machismo that only Wagner could understand. He mellowed the orchestra's hard-diamond glints, shaped and honed its sonorous rumble, and built on it a logical edifice of telling detail and perfect emphasis that could leave even the most indifferent of audiences spellbound. Thus, in

264

CHICAGO TREASURES

one long gush, like a city that survived a siege, the Chicago Symphony came to greatness on a world scale."

85. **In 1969, Chicago added to its skyline the John Hancock Center, one of the most impressive giant buildings of the twentieth century.**

Its unique construction provided not only stability but also a criss-cross design that the city has proudly adopted as a symbol of its own character. At 1,105 feet, it seems to soar even higher, making the sky a partner and friend.

86. **Ruth Page formed the Ruth Page Foundation and School of Dance on the Near North Side in 1970, one of many milestones in her seven decades as a pioneer of distinctively American ballet.**

In the 1920s, Page had been the center of the successful Chicago Allied Arts, a major force on the national scene. As a performer, writer and director, she let neither her advancing age nor traditional taboos stop her from creating true drama on the dance stage.

87. **The musical *Grease* opened in February 1971 at the Kingston Mines Theater, a converted CTA trolley barn.**

Chicagoans Jim Jacobs and Warren Casey wrote the play to celebrate the 1950s, "the decade when nothing happened." It memorializes the DA haircut, cigarette packs rolled up in sleeves, the Pink Ladies, the Burger Palace Boys and the "greased lightnin'" jalopy. It would go on to become a Broadway success and a highly popular movie.

88. **Mike Royko, then of the *Chicago Daily News*, won the 1972 Pulitzer Prize for commentary.**

Mike Royko
(Chicago Tribune)

His column, which was syndicated nationally, demonstrated the acerbic, man-on-the-street wit that made him a Chicago icon. His humor was exemplified in his proposed motto for Chicago: *Ubi est Mea?* or "Where's mine?" He could also be extraordinarily sensitive, as in his annual column about Joseph and the Virgin Mary

being homeless in a modern city. After the *Daily News* folded in 1977, he joined the staff of the *Chicago Sun-Times* and eventually the *Chicago Tribune*.

89. **The Sears Tower was completed in 1974 and, at 1,454 feet, became the world's tallest building.**

The design was extraordinary, using nine framed tubes, each with a cross-section of 75 square feet. The nine tubes rise together for 49 floors; two stop there and two more stop at the 65th floor. In their book *Chicago's Famous Buildings*, Franz Schulze and Kevin Harrington would say, "The bold stepped-back silhouette of the Sears Tower dominates Chicago's skyline with strength and élan."

90. *American Buffalo,* **a drama by young Chicago playwright David Mamet, premiered October 23, 1975.**

Mamet guaranteed the management of the Goodman Theatre that, if they produced his play, it would win the Pulitzer Prize. It did not, but

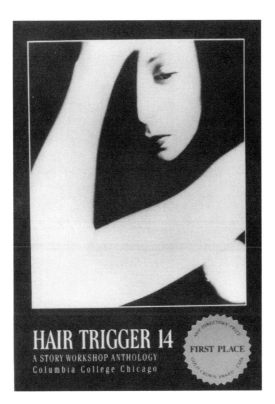

HAIR TRIGGER 14
A STORY WORKSHOP ANTHOLOGY
Columbia College Chicago

FIRST PLACE

it did garner the 1976–77 New York Drama Circle Award. Mamet's Pulitzer would come in 1984 for *Glengarry Glen Ross*. Because of Mamet, New York and Hollywood began to look toward places like Chicago, recognizing that local, intimate theater was a valuable source of talent.

91. **Saul Bellow was awarded the 1976 Nobel Prize for Literature.**

He had also garnered three National Book Awards and the 1974 Pulitzer Prize for fiction. An underlying theme in his writing is the appreciation of reality and details, and how they are woven through everyday life. For him, this theme is often represented by the city of Chicago, which serves as the backdrop for many of his works.

92. **In 1985, *Hair Trigger*, a Columbia College student magazine, won first prize for undergraduate literary magazines from the Coordinating Council of Literary Magazines.**

The *Harvard Advocate* and *Amherst Review* placed second and third. *Hair Trigger* had previously won the award in 1979. The Columbia

University (no connection) Scholastic Press Association would present the publication with its Gold Crown award in 1993 and its Silver Crown award in 1995.

93. *Paco's Story,* written by Chicagoan Larry Heinemann, was the surprise winner of the 1988 National Book Award.

It is a disturbing and powerful story of Vietnam, told by the ghosts of Alpha Company, who haunt Paco, a physically and emotionally disabled survivor of the war.

94. The Chicago Historical Society organized an exhibition, "The Art of Archibald Motley Jr.," which ran from October 23, 1991 through March 17, 1992.

In 1928 Motley had become the first African-American artist to receive a one-man exhibition in a major New York art gallery. He received his formal training at the Art Institute in the days before World War I. His subject matter would include African-Americans, African legends, the rural South, Paris in the 1920s, pool halls as well as street scenes in Chicago's black community, and figures from the Depression-era Works Progress (later Projects) Administration (WPA). "In my paintings," he wrote, "I have tried to paint the Negro as I have seen him and feel him, in myself without adding or detracting, just being frankly honest."

95. In a ceremony September 7, 1995, the Joffrey Ballet, a revered New York institution for 39 years, was welcomed to its new home, Chicago.

The company had not only moved here but also changed its name to the Joffrey Ballet of Chicago. The ballet's troupe of 30 dancers started with a $5 million budget and performed three engagements in Chicago during its first year in the city.

96. Lisel Mueller won the 1997 Pulitzer Prize in poetry for her *Alive Together: New and Selected Poems.*

Ms. Mueller had long been active in poetry circles in the Chicago area. Her work has been described as both "tart and tender." In her youth, she emigrated with her family from Nazi Germany to the Chicago area.

97. The Cultural Center hosted an exhibition called *Capturing Sunlight: The Art of Tree Studios,* from June 18 through September 26, 1999.

This exhibit celebrated the artwork of more than 500 artists who, over the preceding 100 years, had lived and/or worked in Tree Studios. This North Side structure, scheduled to be replaced by commercial development, could have had no better statement of its unique contribution to the city's culture and art than this exhibit. The studios—with skylights, courtyards and great panes of glass with northern exposure—had been designed for arts. One painting on exhibit,

100 EVENTS FROM CHICAGO'S CULTURAL HISTORY

Approaching Storm Threatens Tree Studios, February 25, 1997 by Barton Fiest, was an omen of the troubles to come.

98. On June 13, 2000, Chicago's Bloodshot Records celebrated five years as the pioneer label of insurgent country music with a 2-CD, 40-track anthology, *Down to the Promised Land.*

The new sound bridged the chasm between hard rock and country music by mixing a punk attitude with the song-crafting tradition of country. Bloodshot founders Rob Miller and Nan Warshaw had discovered a growing market, and their burgeoning firm grew larger and more sophisticated in response.

99. The Steppenwolf Theatre Company of Chicago celebrated its 25th anniversary on September 15, 2000.

No other American acting ensemble has survived as long—and thrived as much—as Steppenwolf, recipient of the 1998 National Medal of Arts. Among its prominent members were actors John Malkovich, Gary Sinese, Laurie Metcalf, John Mahoney, Joan Allen, Gary Cole and Amy Morton.

100. On December 11, 2000, the $46 million Goodman Theater Complex opened at Randolph and Dearborn Streets.

Located in the North Loop area, the theater would anchor the newly-developed Theater District. The opening climaxed a 75-year history during which the Goodman provided nationally recognized local theater. With a list of writers and directors in recent years that has included John Reich, William Woodman, Gregory Mosher, David Mamet and Robert Falls, the Goodman has drawn greatly on the talents produced by the many innovative Off-Loop Chicago theaters.

INDEX

BEAUTY IS

REFLECTED IN THE EYES OF US ALL

We want to know where and why you find beauty in Chicago and the Chicago Wilderness. Please write or e-mail us your thoughts in a sentence or short paragraph, and we may share your visions of beauty in an updated edition of this book.

Kenan Heise
c/o Bonus Books
160 East Illinois Street
Chicago, IL 60611
kheise@bonus-books.com